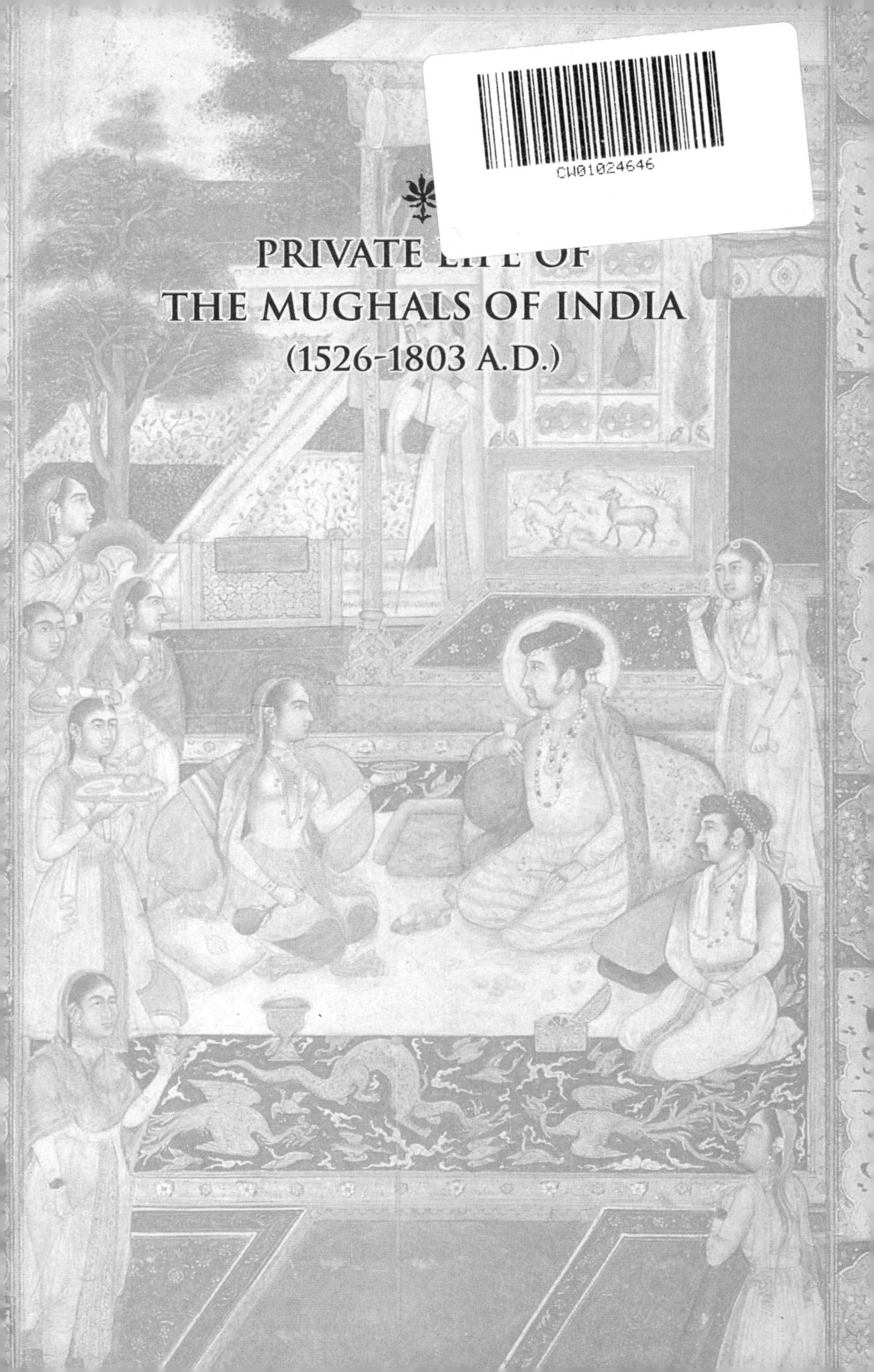

PRIVATE LIFE OF THE MUGHALS OF INDIA (1526-1803 A.D.)

PRIVATE LIFE OF THE MUGHALS OF INDIA (1526-1803 A.D.)

R. NATH

Rupa & Co

Published 2005 by
Rupa & Co
7/16, Ansari Road, Daryaganj
New Delhi 110 002

Sales Centres:
Allahabad Bangalore Chandigarh
Chennai Hyderabad Jaipur
Kathmandu Kolkata Mumbai Pune

Cover &Book Design by
Kapil Gupta
kapilkgupta@hotmail.com

Printed in India by
Gopsons Paper Ltd
A-14 Sector 60
Noida 201 301

CONTENTS

Preface 7

1. **The Mughal *Harem*** 10
   - (a) Architectural disposition 12
   - (b) Underground complex 16
   - (c) Institutional organisation 19
2. **The Ladies of the Mughal *Harem*** 24
   - (a) Ladies of Babur and Humayun 25
   - (b) Akbar's *Harem* 26
   - (c) Jehangir's *Harem* 29
   - (d) Nur Jehan Begum 33
   - (e) Anarkali 35
   - (f) The Lady of the Taj 36
3. **Rajput Wives of the Mughals** 40
4. **Administration of the Mughal *Harem*** 52
5. **Circumcision among the Muslims** 64
   - (a) The rite of Circumcision 64
   - (b) Discontinuity of circumcision by the Mughals 71
6. **Mughal Kitchen, Dining Etiquette & Cuisine** 81
   - (a) Management of the Kitchen 82
   - (b) System of Service 90
   - (c) Mughal Cuisine 93
7. **Mughal Perfumes & Incenses** 108
8. **Mughal Addictions and Intoxicants** 115
   - (a) Wine and Opium 115
   - (b) Tobacco and *Huqah* 122
   - (c) *Pan* (Betel-leaf) 125

9. **Medicines and Aphrodisiacal Drugs** 128

(a) Preliminary Medicines 130

(b) Aphrodisiacal Drugs: *Dravana* 137

(c) *Stambhana* Drugs 140

(d) *Vajikarana* Drugs 142

(e) *Auparishtaka* Means 144

10. **Mughal Amusements and Pastimes** 154

(a) Functions and Ceremonies 155

(b) *Mina Bazar* 156

(c) Amusements (Indoor Games) 158

(d) Cultural, Artistic and Playful Engagements 165

11. **Illumination (Lighting) of the Mughal Palace** 170

12. **Imperial Paraphernalia** 176

(a) Floor Coverings etc. 177

(b) *Farrash-Khanah* 180

(c) Wardrobe (*Kurkyaraq* or *Karkaraq-Khanah*) 189

(d) Shawls and Stuffs 195

(e) Precious Stones and Jewellery 203

13. **Daily Routine of the Mughal Emperors** 207

Detail of Colour Plates 215

Index 217

PREFACE

Titled as it is, the book deals with the little known, but much scandalised, private life of the Mughals who ruled from 1526, practically to 1803 when the British captured Delhi and Agra, their nerve-centres, from them. This included the period of the reign of three great Mughals, viz. Akbar (1556-1605), Jehangir (1605-27) and Shah Jehan (1628-58), of little more than a century. They possessed not only fabulous wealth, but also the vision to found a *culture-state,* in the real sense of the term. Planting it in the soil as naturally as a banyan tree, they institutionalised their life, as much as their government. The former, almost completely shrouded in mystery, offers one of the most interesting aspects of medieval Indian history and culture.

Unfortunately, the official record of their day to day living which was scrupulously maintained has been lost to us.

It has been generally believed that the contemporary Persian chroniclers, living under the court patronage as they did, have blacked out this aspect of their history. Consequently, the modern historians who have ventured to write on this subject, i.e. Mughal *harem* life, have almost entirely depended and drew on accounts of foreign travellers. These European travellers visited the Mughal empire contemporarily and some of them were received by the Great Mughals. But they had limitations of language, culture and accessibility to correct information. They viewed the things from the point of view of European civilisation and were easily tempted to misinterpret, exaggerate and scandalise. Their narratives on Mughal life have, thus, come up to be a strange mixture of a tiny fact with a mountain of fiction. Our historians who, unfortunately relied on their travelogues, have also erred in a large measure and have tremendously contributed to the misunderstanding and misrepresentation of the Mughal lifestyle. It has been unduly romanticised.

Truly, the Persian chroniclers were either prevented from knowing what happened within the four walls of the Mughal *harem* owing to strict protocol and *purdah*, or even when they had access to this knowledge, they did not have the courage to write on this sensitive subject. The Mughal life, consequently, remained a closely guarded secret.

However, the human nature being what it is, these contemporary intellectuals' sense of wonder led them to leave clever references to their private life in a word or two, casually, in historical narratives, and one has just to read between the lines. A lifetime's rapport with these sources is needed to unravel these mysteries and, towards the end of it, one is simply amazed to see that there is probably nothing which was not known and which has not been recorded.

Thus, for example, when the historian Badaoni stated, on the eve of Akbar's marriage with the princess of Jaisalmer, that she 'obtained eternal glory by entering the female apartments', he artfully recorded that the Mughals did not practice divorce, or separation even by death, and they married for 'eternity', which is how the institution of *Sohagpura* (The House of Eternal Matrimony) came into being. One has just to live up with them to be able to write an authentic history on this abstract subject.

Thus does it cover such aspects of their living as food and drinks; clothes and ornaments; perfumes and incenses; addictions and intoxicants; amusements and pastimes; floor-coverings, furniture and lighting; and, of course, their sex life to which a few chapters have been devoted. How the Mughal king managed to keep a few hundred young and beautiful women attached to his bed is as enlightening a study as it is interesting.

Though based on research, it is written without its jargon, in a simple, readable form, for the general reader.

Jaipur — R. NATH

1
The Mughal Harem

The seclusion of women was enjoined in the *Quran* (XXXIII. 55) and it was the rule for respectable Muslim women to remain secluded at home, and not to travel abroad unveiled, nor to associate with men other than their husbands or such male relatives as are forbidden in marriage by reason of consanguinity. In consequence of these injunctions, which had all the force of a divine enactment, the females of a Muslim family resided in apartments which were in an enclosed courtyard and excluded from public view. This enclosure was called the *harem*.

The term *harem* was derived from the Arabic *harem* (literally, something sacred or forbidden); or Persian *harem* (sanctuary). Sanskrit *harmya* also means palace. It denoted seraglio, or the secluded part of the palace or residence reserved for the ladies of the Muslim household. It was also called *zenanah; harem-sara; harem-gah; mahal-sara;* and *raniwas.* Later, it was called *zenani-dyodhi* in the Rajput states. The chief officer of the *harem* was accordingly called *Nazir; Nazir-i-Mahal; Nazir-i-Mashkuyah* (Incharge of women's quarters) and, most popularly, *Khwajah-sara* (discussed in a following chapter).

The Mughal *harem* consisted of a large number of women of different regions, coming from different cultural milieus, speaking different languages. They were kept in strict seclusion and *purdah* within the four walls of the complex and their relationship with the outside world was completely severed and the proverb that a woman entered the *harem* by *doli* (bridal palanquin) and left it by *arthi* or *janaza* (funeral bier) was literally true. No male, except the king, was allowed to go into the *harem* and entry was barred even to his grown-up sons. It was a very sensitive matter and its organisation was, therefore, extremely difficult and complicated. It goes to the credit of the Mughals that they could manage their *harem* efficiently and in an orderly way. It was Akbar (the Great Mughal who ruled from 1556 to 1605 A.D.), indeed, who founded the customs, traditions and institutions which guided and regulated the course of the Mughal life and culture. These were faithfully and scrupulously followed by his descendants; Jehangir (1605-27); Shah Jehan (1628-58); Aurangzeb (1658-1707) and the later Mughals (1707-1803). Abu'l Fazl, author of *Ain-i-Akbari,* has recorded that Akbar raised faithful persons to several ranks in the service of the seraglio. Trust was the criterion and only the most trustworthy persons could be appointed to the *harem* duties, so sensitive was this matter. There was a hierarchy of officers, to ensure checks and balances and, above all, the king himself looked into every detail related to it and maintained a personal watch on its day to day working.

(a) Architectural disposition

The Mughal *harem* was a large complex enclosed by high walls, with fine buildings inside. It was architecturally so planned as to ensure as much healthy living as segregation and *purdah*. A vast court (*chowk; angan*) open to sky was invariably situated in the centre of the complex. It is there in the Agra Fort and Fatehpur Sikri. Sometimes, there were several courts laid out with spacious gardens. Double-storeyed annexes were built on its two or four sides and, in fact, all of them opened on the central court, thus drawing the light and air on it. The *harem* inmates assembled in this court on festive occasions and it was the pivot of the *harem* life. Each annexe also had its own court open to sky and also a garden with such water-devices as tanks, channels and fountains where the ladies

1. Open spaces (court and verandah) Rang-Mahal, Fatehpur Sikri

2. Open spaces (court and verandah) Rang-Mahal, Fatehpur Sikri

could retire and relax. These suites were interconnected by covered passages. Spacious terraces with beautiful *jali* balustrades on the edges and intermittantly disposed *chhatris* and *chhaparkhats* were provided on the first floor, as are there in the Raniwas at Fatehpur Sikri, and upper floors in multi-storeyed palaces to enable them to view the landscape and the gardens below. In any case, there were adequate open spaces inside the *harem* (plates 1 to 5).

3. Open spaces (court; verandah and terraces) Raniwas, Fatehpur Sikri

4. Open spaces (court; verandah and terraces) Raniwas, Fatehpur Sikri

Each annexe was provided with a toilet-system of its own. Toilets were also provided on one side of the complex as a whole. They were either in the form of *hammams* (where latrine and bathroom both were provided together), or in series of latrines given at the edge of the complex, adequately secured by high walls, the remains of which have survived in the *harem* quarters of Agra Fort. (Fig. 1). Latrines were cleaned by scavenging. An underground tunnel, nearly six feet

5. Verandah (dalan), Raniwas, Fatehpur Sikri

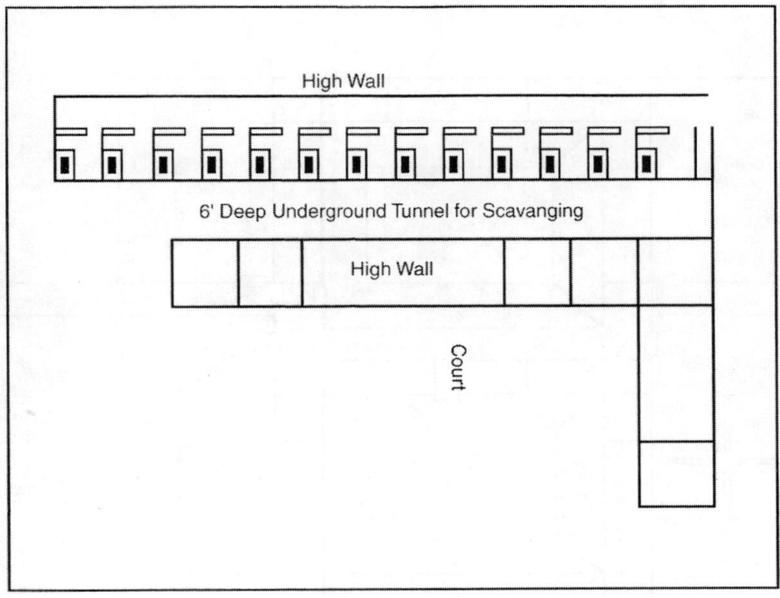

Fig. 1. Plan of the Toilet System in the Mughal Harem

high, was provided below these latrines for the use of the female scavengers. The entire latrine cell was built of thick brick masonry, the main hole being made in a six to eight inch thick stone slab, to ensure security. In such a case as this, provision for a bathroom was made separately in each annexe or apartment. Generally, a full double-storeyed annexe, with its own court, garden and sets of *dalans* (verandahs), rooms and chambers (Fig. 2) was allotted to a queen (*begum*) or concubine each, so that she could live there along with her own maids whom she either brought from her father's household, or bought from the market, or received as a gift from the king, for her exclusive use. It is noteworthy that all these suites and apartments were interconnected by narrow corridors and passages. These were, in fact, the lifeline of the *harem* and it was through them that it was controlled and maintained. There was no outlet except the main gate which was most vigilantly guarded round the clock.

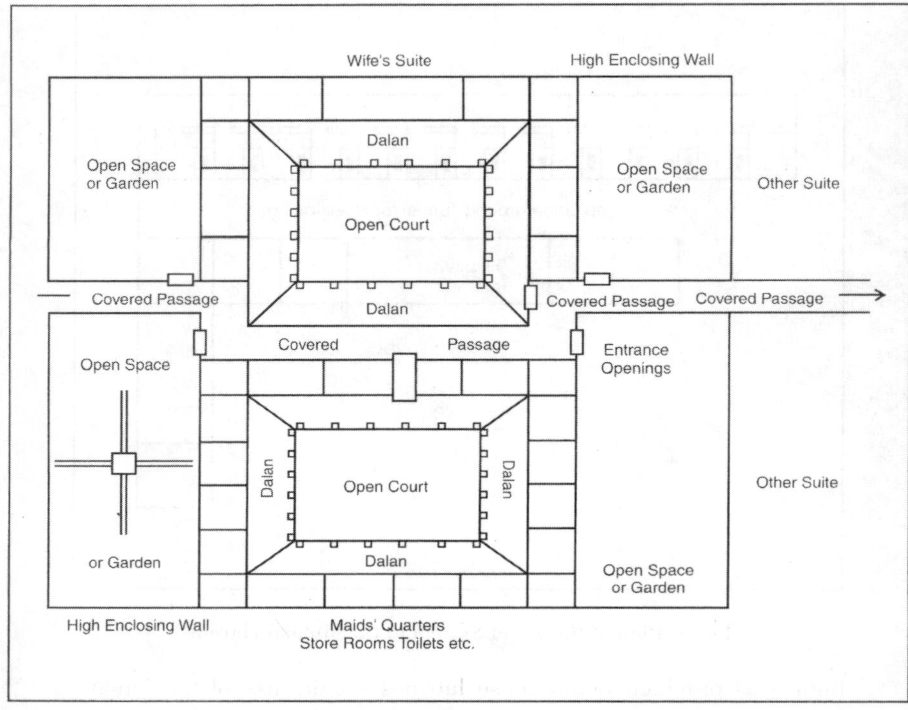

Fig. 2. Plan of a Queen's Suite in the Mughal Harem

Every effort was made to provide for the comforts of the princesses of the *harem*. Besides the open spaces through courts and terraces, flower-parterres and tree-lined avenues of the gardens and swimming pools were also made inside the palace for the ladies to relax, enjoy and live a healthy life.

(b) Underground complex

The most important feature of the architecture of the Mughal *harem* was, however, its system of 'underground' chambers, corridors and stairways, which secretly opened in all its buildings. This has survived intact in the Agra Fort, in several storeys in the basement of the Akbari-Mahal and the Jehangiri-Mahal. There was a long,

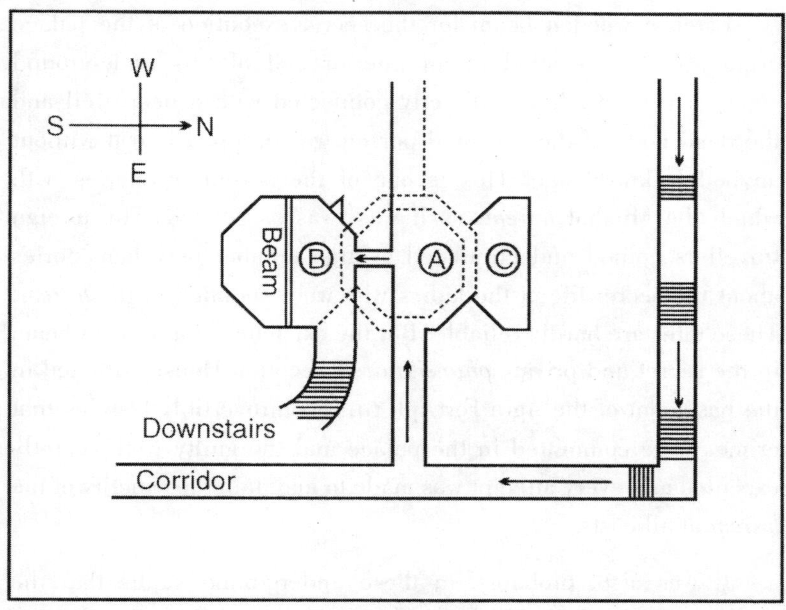

Fig. 3. Phansighar Plan, Agra Fort

through corridor, with ventilators given on the riverside, running from one end of the *harem* to the other. Stairways, intermittently provided in it, secretly led to different annexes. It was through it that the *harem* inmates could be surprised at any moment and a strict surveillance maintained. This corridor was exclusively used by the king himself, and, that is why, his historians noted that the king had such supernatural powers that he could appear anywhere in the palace at any time. It was through this basement complex that this was possible. The chambers situated in this complex were provided with tanks, cascades and fountains. These were extremely cool in the summer season and, possibly, used for repose by the king along with his choicest women. It was, in fact, through this ingenious architectural organisation of the *harem* that the Mughals managed and maintained it.

Later, a wooden beam for the secret execution of the palace criminals was installed in an interior cell of this underground complex (Fig. 3). It was directly connected with a deep well and the dead body of the executed person was dropped into it without anybody's knowledge. This is one of the several mysteries with which the Mughal *harem*, as it was, was associated. The foreign travellers coined and circulated a large number of vulgar stories about the secret life of the ladies who were confined in the *harem*. These tales are hardly reliable. But the existence of a wooden beam in the secret and private *phansighar* (Execution House) situated in the basement of the Agra Fort (pl. 6), incontrovertibly testifies that crimes were committed in the palace and the guilty were secretly executed and every attempt was made to maintain the sanctity of the *harem* at all costs.

It was also, probably, in these underground vaults that the treasures of the great Mughals were buried. Shah Jehan's historian Lahauri and the contemporary French traveller Tavernier have left

6. Wooden Beam of the Underground Phansighar (Execution-House); Agra Fort

records of these treasure vaults. Agra Fort was the seat of the Mughal empire for about a century and abundant treasures were kept ready at hand. These were kept in these basement apartments connected by tunnels within access of the king and his trusted nobles and servants. That the Great Mughals from Akbar to Shah Jehan possessed fabulous wealth which invited the envy of the world's greatest monarchies is a historical fact.

(c) Institutional organisation

Though several thousand women lived in the *harem*—by Abu'l Fazl's record there were more than five thousand in Akbar's *harem*—they were systematically lodged in separate apartments. *Harem* was divided into sections which were judiciously allotted. Personal maids lived with the queen in her own quarter, otherwise women servants who were kept to perform different duties of the *harem*, e.g. cleaning and sweeping the floors; lighting; maintenance of curtains, carpets and furniture; gardening; service; entertainment etc. lived in separate quarters in the *harem*. It is a general misconception that every woman of the Mughal *harem* served a sexual purpose. Hardly five percent of them were queens (*begums*), concubines and slave-girls of the king and had access to his bed, others were just maid-servants employed to serve them in particular, and for the maintenance and upkeep of the *harem* in general. They too were, however, subjected to the same discipline of seclusion and *purdah* and it was here that their femininity was suppressed and circumvented.

Chaste women were appointed as *daroghas* (supervising officers) and superintendents over each section. One was entrusted with the duties of the writer (*nawis*). Thus, like the Mughal *daftar* (office), *harem* also functioned in proper order. The salaries of the ladies of the *harem*, one and all, were fixed. These were sufficiently liberal. We have figures of Akbar's *harem*. Not counting the presents which the king generously bestowed, the women of the highest rank received from Rs. 1610 to 1028 per month. Looking at the cheapness of things in that age when gold was sold at Rs. 10 per *tola* = 11.66 grams, and an average family could live decently at Rs. 5 per month, these were fabulous figures and enabled them to spend munificently on charities and buildings, over and above their own costumes and ornaments. Some maidservants received from Rs. 51 to 20 per month, while others from Rs. 40 to 2 per month only, in accordance with the nature of the duties which were, of course, assigned to them on the basis of their experience and expertise. Attached to the *Diwan-i-Khanah-i-Khas* (Private Audience Hall of the Palace or *Harem*) was a clever and zealous writer (*nawis*) who superintended the expenditure of the *harem* and kept an account of its cash and stores. Everything was systematically executed and the record of everything was duly maintained. If a woman wanted anything, within the limits of her salary, she applied to one of the *tahwildars* (cash-keepers) of the *harem*. The *tahwildar* sent a requisition to the writer who checked it and forwarded it to the general treasurer who made the payment in cash.

The writer also made out an estimate of the annual expenditure of the *harem* establishment and prepared a summary receipt. It was countersigned by the ministers of the state. It was then stamped with a peculiar imperial seal which was used only in grants connected with the *harem*, when it became payable. The money was paid by the cash-keeper of the general treasury to the general *tahwildar* who, on the order of the writer of the *harem*, handed it over to several *tahwildars* for distribution among the servants of the seraglio. All amounts were reckoned to their salaries at the current rate of 40 *dams* per *rupiya* (rupee). It is noteworthy that these payment officers were male and they were not allowed to go into the *harem*. The requisitions were, therefore, sent through the maidservants and eunuchs. They gradually acquired expertise in dealing with the officialdom and began to charge a *dasturi* (commission) which never exceeded a *dam* per rupee. *Dasturi* was later institutionalised in the affairs of the Mughal state.

There were several other officers of the imperial household, which was a separate department for all practical purposes, as important as any other department of the state. A large number of household duties were performed by the *Mir-i-Saman* (literally, incharge of stores) who was later upgraded and designated *Khan-i-Saman* (Lord of Stores). This office was reduced to *khansama* and corrupted to denote just a menial cook-cum-butler during the early British period when every attempt was made to degrade, denigrate, denounce and defame the Mughal legacy. This biased British attitude has continued to guide our historians to this day and we owe many of the popular misunderstandings to it.

The inside of the *harem* was guarded vigilantly, round the clock, by sober, strongly-built and tough women who were generally requisitioned for the guard duty itself from Tartary, central Asia and Afghanistan. They were not well-conversant with the *deshi* (vernacular) dialects which were mainly spoken in the *harem*, there being a large number of indigenous women in it. This prevented them from communicating freely with the inmates of the *harem* and allowed them to maintain a safe distance. Deaf and dumb maids were also employed. Fear of condign punishment, even on slight dereliction of duty, deterred them from being soft and sympathetic to the ladies, a number of whom were kept there against their will. They are recorded to be rough and ruthless. Still cases of bribery were reported, mostly during the period of the later Mughals. These guard-women were directly responsible to the *Khwajasara*, the highest officer of the *harem* establishment and, hence, they could not be bullied even by the queens. The most trustworthy of them were placed about the apartments of the king where he reposed. His life was the most precious thing in the empire and he had to be guarded most scrupulously. That is why only a person of proven loyalty in whom the king could repose total faith was appointed the *khwaja-sara* of the *harem*.

Eunuchs (*mukhannis;* castrated men) were placed outside the enclosure of the *harem*, and they were also not allowed, normally, to enter it. But they were an important link between the maids of the queens and the officers of the *harem* as the former were not supposed to meet the latter themselves. It was only at a later stage, during the declining period of the later Mughals, that eunuchs took over the control of the *harem* and became its dominant functionaries. At a proper distance from them, was maintained, day and night, a guard of faithful Rajputs. Beyond them waited the porters of the gates. Besides, on all the four sides, there were guards of the nobles (*mansabdars*) on *chowki* (watch) duty, *Ahadis* (Imperial Troops) and other troops, according to their ranks. They were divided into seven parts, each of whom was appointed to this duty for one day of the week under the superintendence of a trustworthy *mansabdar* (noble) who was called *Mir-Mahal* (Commander of the Palace). An equally important officer attached to the guard duty was *Mir-Arz* (Incharge of Petitions) who was fully acquainted with the protocol. All orders of the king were made known through these two officers who were in attendance about the palace, day and night, ready to receive the orders. *Chowki* was affected in the most organised and disciplined manner to ensure greatest security of the person of the king, as much as the sanctity of the *harem*. This system continued during the period of the Great Mughals and deteriorated only after the death of Aurangzeb in 1707 A.D.

Entry into and exit from the *harem* was carefully regulated and recorded, and there were a number of checks and balances which rendered the system almost foolproof. Whenever *begums*, or the wives of nobles, or other women of chaste character, desired to be presented (in the *harem*), they first notified their wish to the servants of the *harem*, and waited for a reply. From thence, they sent their request to the officers of the palace, after which those who were eligible, i.e. those who were found fit for entry, were permitted to enter the *harem*. Some women of rank were granted permission to stay in the *harem* even for a month. Such was the sensitive nature of the *harem* that the king, notwithstanding the great number of faithful guards, maintained his personal vigilance on it, with the help of his own spies and informers, and an efficient system of underground corridors and stairways, and kept it in perfect order.

The Mughal *harem* also travelled with the king on long distance journeys, like his treasures, in accordance with the dictates of the Mughal polity. Jehangir, for example, was constantly on the move from Agra to Delhi – Lahore – Kabul and back; again from Agra to Ajmer – Ahmedabad – Ujjain – Mandu and back; and he spent the last few years of his reign travelling between Lahore and Kashmir. His *harem* moved with him. The ladies travelled in litters or covered palanquins; curtained *bahals* and *raths* (carriages drawn by bullocks) and *chaukhandis* (covered litters) placed on camels and elephants. Imperial carriages were invariably covered and nobody was allowed to come close to them, so rigid was the system of *purdah* imposed upon the royal ladies. Akbar invented a large carriage, drawn by an elephant which was spacious enough to hold, besides sleeping apartments, several bathrooms. While on journeys, the Mughal king lived in camp, in extremely gorgeous tents of a wide variety. On all encampments, a separate quarter was reserved and secluded for the imperial seraglio. It was adequately enclosed by *sarapardas* (*qanats* = high padded curtains) and strictly guarded. The ladies had a change of climate and environment and they lived as comfortably and securely in the camp as in the palace.

2

The Ladies of the Mughal Harem

The Mughals were Sunni Muslims and, at least theoretically, they believed in the orthodox religion of Islam. The *Shariat* allowed a faithful to have a maximum of four wives by *nikah* (legal marriage contract). But the conditions of the medieval ages were different. Women were considered a prized war-booty and they were also easily available in slave-market. The people, therefore, were polygamous and the rich among them could even afford to have more than four wives. Hence arose the system of *mut'ah* marriages (contracted for a limited period for a certain sum of money). Besides these two types of wives, the powerful nobles also kept a large number of young and beautiful concubines and slave-girls for their pleasure. All laws, indeed, are made for the poor; the rich observe them more in their breach.

It may be noted, however, that what is licentiousness today, was a mark of social status during the medieval ages and modern criterion cannot be applied on history. Mirza 'Aziz Koka's famous proverb that a man should marry four wives: a Persian to have somebody to talk to and make love; a Khurasani to do the house-work; a Hindu to caress the husband and nurse the children; and a woman of Mawar-un-Nahr to have someone to whip as a warning for the other three, shows how the medieval people fancied to have four wives from different regions.

(a) Ladies of Babur and Humayun

Babur, the founder of the Mughal dynasty in India, is recorded to have had more than four wives at a time. The most prominent among them were—Ayisha Sultan Begum Miranshahi (his first wife); Zainab; Ma'suma Sultan Begum; Maham Begum (mother of his son and successor Humayun); Gulrukh Begchik Begum (mother of his two sons Kamran and Askari); Dildar Begum (mother of his son Hindal and daughter Gulbadan); Bibi Mubarika; Gul-Nar Aghacha and Nar-Gul. Humayun also had more than four wives and Bega (Haji) Begum; Hamida Banu Begum (mother of his son and successor Akbar); Mah-Chuchak Begum; Gunwar Bibi; Gul-Barg Barlas; Maywa-Jan; Shad Bibi and Shaham Agha have been named, besides a number of unnamed concubines. But, both of them led a very tough and turbulent life. They were constantly on the move and in action, either in the battlefield, or on journeys from place to place, some time from country to country. They could not lead a stable, settled life and mostly lived in the camp.

The set, group, team or collection of the ladies (wives and concubines) of either Babur or Humayun, who travelled and lived with him in camps under extremely difficult and impoverished conditions, was not, technically, a *harem*. It was not an institution and it was not an organised house, with its own rules and norms, and a hierarchy of officials to manage it.

(b) Akbar's *Harem*

Harem as an institution was founded and developed, in the right sense of the term, by Akbar and it was under him that it worked systematically and independently like any other department of the government. Whether in an architecture or camp, it had a fixed budget and a hierarchy of officials; a kitchen, a system of lighting and other paraphernalia; and a set of regulations to guide its standard working. Above all, it ensured inviolable *purdah* and seclusion of the ladies and maintained, what was termed, its sanctity for the exclusive satisfaction of the king. This was its objective, which was less guided by the *Shariat* injunction on *purdah* and more by its need, efficacy and use during the medieval times. Orthodox injuction to restrict *nikah* marriages to four was altogether ignored and the Mughal king contracted marriages freely, and unencumbered by any law, human or divine.

More interesting is the fact that Akbar married a lady for eternity as the Hindus did, and he never practised *talaq* (which was something below his imperial dignity). A lady was admitted into his *harem* forever, hence the proverbial *doli-arthi* (bridal palanquin to funeral bier) concept of her marital status. This was carried forward to such an extent that even the widows of the deceased king were not allowed to remarry and they spent their remaining life in a separate garden-enclosure called *Sohagpura* (literally, the palace of eternal marital bliss = *suhag;* or the house of eternal matrimony). It existed on the bank of the river Yamuna at Agra in between the palaces of

Wazir Khan and I'tibar Khan and was noticed by Pelsaert, the Dutch factor who was living in the city from 1620 to 1627. It was a large enclosure where the widows (queens and concubines) of the late king were lodged together, in complete segregation and strict seclusion. Gradually, it assumed the status and dignity of an institution. This shows that the widows of the late king were not allowed either to commit *sati* or remarry and they were all confined, for the rest of their life, except the mother of the present king, to a palace reserved for them, separately from the royal *harem*. They were obviously provided with handsome stipends. Like the Mughal *harem*, this was also a closely guarded secret.

Akbar raised Mughal kingship to a divine status and his *harem* too, therefore, could not remain on the level of the ordinary mortals who restricted themselves to four wives and practised divorce. Marriage with the Mughal king was deemed to be an act of divine grace which could not be surrendered even after his death. Hence, the sanctity attached to the Mughal *harem*, which was not an ordinary house for the living of the ladies, but a thoroughly organised and mythified imperial institution.

Akbar passed benevolent laws regulating marriages of the commoners. Marriage before the age of puberty was prohibited. Consent of the bride and bridegroom, along with the permission of the parents, was made mandatory in a marriage contract. Marriage between near relations was restricted. High dowries were disapproved. Normally, people were discouraged to marry more than one wife, both for financial and health reasons. These reformatory measures show how ahead of his times Akbar was.

He appointed two sober and sensible officers called *Tu'i-Begi* (Masters of Marriages) to inquire into the circumstances of the prospective bride and bridegroom respectively, in order to regulate marriages. Sometimes only one officer performed these duties. A marriage-tax was also collected by the state from both the contracting parties at the following rate:

Mansabdars of		*Rate of Tax*
5000 to 1000	–	10 gold *muhrs* (each of one *tola*)
1000 to 500	–	4 gold *muhrs*
500 to 100	–	2 gold *muhrs*
100 to 40	–	1 gold *muhr*
40 to 10	–	4 silver *rupiya* (rupees)
	–	(10 *rupiya* = gold *muhr*)
Rich People	–	4 silver *rupiya*
Middle Class	–	1 silver *rupiya*
Commoners	–	1 *dam* (40 *dam* = 1 *rupiya*)

These measures were intended to regulate the marriages of his subjects.

Though Akbar never indulged in excessive sex, he had a taste for young beautiful women whose company he liked. He had in his *harem* a large number of handsome concubines and slave-girls for his pleasure, besides more than a dozen legally married wives. Names of some of his wives as Sultan Ruqayyah Begum (his first wife); Sultan Salima Begum; so-called daughter of Raja Bharmal Kachhwaha of Amer (mother of his son and successor Jehangir); beautiful wife of Abu'l Wasi (who was forced to divorce her to enable Akbar to marry her); Bibi Daulat Shad; a daughter of Abdullah Khan Mughul; a daughter of Miran Mubarak Shah of Khandesh etc., have been recorded. These marriages were mostly contracted to reinforce and strengthen the alliances with the chieftains of different regions and these were, essentially, political marriages. Pretty slave-girls were purchased from the slave market and presented to the king like any other commodity. The most beautiful and cultured of them were retained in the Mughal *harem,* trained and drafted in his personal service. Some who succeeded in winning over the heart of the king were raised to the status of concubines, within the definition of *mut'ah* marriage, and bore him children. Normally, the king considered it below his imperial dignity to cohabit with a slave-girl until he raised her to some sort of honourable status. In fact, these polygamous people were not as promiscuous as we misunderstand them to be, in accordance with our notions determined by modern privations. Sex was munificently available and the choice was not between sex and no-sex as it is today (which is why rape is so rampant), it was for the excellent one. Naturally, the lady who entered the Mughal *harem* as a consequence of political alliance but was not very beautiful, had rare access to the imperial bed, after the consummation of the marriage. She was virtually forgotten to lead a miserable life within the *harem* precincts ever after. There was no law on earth to rescue her.

(c) Jehangir's *harem*

Jehangir was a sensuous person and he excessively indulged both in wine and women. Even as a prince, he is recorded to have more than twenty wives when he was only twenty seven years old. Man Bai, daughter of Raja Bhagwandas of Amer (Ambar) was his first wife whom he married in 1585, when he was barely fifteen. She gave birth to a daughter Sultan-un-Nisa Begum in 1586 and a son, the unfortunate Khusrau, in 1587. She was then given the title, *Shah Begum.* He married Jodh Bai, later entitled *Jagat Gosain* daughter of Mota Raja Udai Singh of Jodhpur in 1586. She gave birth to a son, Khurram (Shah Jehan). He also married a daughter of Rai Raisingh of Bikaner and a daughter of Sa'id Khan Ghakkhar the same year. He married sixteen other ladies during the next ten years, the most prominent of whom were: *Sahib-i-Jamal,* daughter of Khwajah

Hasan; *Malika-i-Jehan* daughter of Kalyan Mal of Jaisalmer; Nur-un-Nisa Begum, sister of Muzaffar Husain; Saliha Banu Begum alias *Padshah-Mahal;* Karamsi, daughter of Raja Kesu Das Rathor; daughter of Ali Rai, ruler of Little Tibet; daughter of Mubarak Chak of Kashmir; daughter of Husain Chak of Kashmir; daughter of the king of Khandesh; daughter of Khwajah Jahan-i-Kabul; and daughter of Mirza Sarjar. A large number of children were born to him, though most of them died in infancy. This shows a great sexual activity on the part of the young crown prince, by any standard. These marriages had exceeded the prescribed limit of four legal *nikah* matrimonies and these were extra marriages. These were contracted mostly to cement political alliances. After his accession to the throne in 1605, he further married a daughter of Jagat Singh, daughter of Ramchandra Bundela and, finally, Mihr-un-Nisa, the famous Nur Jehan Begum, in 1611. Besides these legally married wives, he also had a large number of concubines who too were bearing children for him. Two sons Jahandar and Shahriyar were thus born of concubines. By a rough estimate, he had nearly 300 young and beautiful women attached to his bed, an incomprehensible figure in the modern age. This shows his over-indulgence in sex and his excessive engagement in the *harem*.

Pelsaert, the Dutch factor who was a contemporary of Jehangir and an eye-witness to the early 17th century Mughal life and culture, has left a general comment on the private life of the king and his nobles (who emulated him). Thus did he note,

> Their *mahals* are adorned internally with lascivious sensuality, wanton and reckless festivity, superfluous pomp, inflated pride, and ornamental daintiness, while the servants of the lords may justly be described as a generation of iniquity, greed and oppression, for, like their masters,

they make hay while the sun shines. Sometimes while they think they are exalted to a seat in heaven, an envious report to the king may cast them down to the depths of woe. Very few of them, however, think of the future, but they enjoy themselves to the uttermost while they can. As a rule they have three or four wives, the daughters of worthy men, but the senior wife commands most respect. All live together in the enclosure surrounded by high walls, which is called the *mahal,* having tanks and gardens inside. Each wife has separate apartments for herself and her slaves of whom there may be ten, or twenty or 100, according to her fortune. Each has a regular monthly allowance for her expenditure. Jewels and clothes are provided by the husband according to the extent of his affection. Their food comes from one kitchen, but each wife takes it in her own apartments; for they hate each other secretly, though they seldom or never allow it to be seen, because of their desire to retain the favour of their husband, whom they fear, honour, and worship as a god rather than a man. Each night he visits a particular wife, or *mahal,* and receives a very warm welcome from her and from the slaves, who, dressed specially for the occasion, seem to fly, rather than run about their duties. If it is the hot weather, they undress the husband as soon as he comes in, and rub his body with pounded sandalwood and rosewater, or some other scented and cooling oil. Fans are kept going steadily in the room, or in the open air, where they usually sit. Some of the slaves chafe the master's hands and feet, some sit and sing, or play music and dance, or provide other recreation, the wife sitting near him all the time. They study night and day how to make exciting perfumes and efficacious preserves such as *mosseri* and *faloni,* containing amber, pearls, gold opium and other stimulants; but these are mostly for their own use, for they eat them occasionally in the day-time, because they produce a pleasant elevation of the spirit. In the cool of the evening they drink a great deal of wine, for the women learn the habit quickly from their husbands, and drinking has become very fashionable in the last few years. The husband sits like a golden cock among the gilded hens until midnight, or until passion, or drink, sends him to bed. Then if one of the pretty slave-girls takes his fancy, he calls her to him and enjoys her, his wife not daring to show any signs of displeasure, but dissembling, though she will take it out of the slave-girls later on. Two or three eunuchs or more, who are merely purchased Bengali slaves, but are usually faithful to their master, are appointed for each wife, to ensure that she is seen by no man except her husband; and, if a eunuch fails in this duty, he, with everyone else to blame for the stranger's presence, is in danger of losing his life. They are thus held in high esteem by their master, but the women pay them still greater regard, for the whole management of the *mahal* is in their hands, and they can give or refuse whatever is wanted. Thus they can get whatever they desire—fine horses to ride, servants to attend them outside, and female slaves inside the house, clothes as fine and smart as those of their master himself. The wives feel themselves bound to do all this, in order that what happens in the house may be concealed from their husband's knowledge; for many, or perhaps most of them, so far forget themselves, that, when their husband has gone away, either to court, or to some place where he takes only his favourite wife, and leaves the rest at home, they allow the eunuch to enjoy them according to his ability, and thus gratify their burning passions when they have no opportunity of going out; but otherwise they spare no craft or trouble to

> enable them to enjoy themselves outside. These wretched women wear, indeed, the most expensive clothes, eat the daintiest food, and enjoy all worldly pleasures except one, and for that one they grieve, saying they would willingly give everything in exchange for a beggar's poverty.

He does not name anybody and this is just his observation and opinion on a noble's *harem*, which as an eye-witness's narrative has some weight. However, the Mughal *harem* was a very delicate matter and a sweeping generalisation is hardly justified. While the Persian chroniclers could not dare to write on this subject, the account of foreign travellers are, by and large, a strange mixture of facts and fiction owing mainly to their limitations of language, culture and accessibility to correct information and it is only with the greatest caution that their romantic tales can be used for making history. Their general comments, however, give an idea of the conditions which prevailed in that age.

(d) Nur Jehan Begum

Nur Jehan is perhaps the most romantic and famous name among the Mughal ladies. She was the daughter of Mirza Ghiyath Beg, a polished and cultured Iranian noble who migrated to India and was admitted into the imperial service. She was born in 1577 and named Mihr-un-Nisa. She grew to become an extremely beautiful, talented and cultured girl. Prince Salim (Jehangir) loved her and he developed a desire to possess her. But Akbar believed only in politically advantageous marriages and he had no soft corner for romances. She was a Shiah and he did not allow the heir apparent to marry Mihr-un-Nisa in spite of his irrepressible longing for her and, just to ward off the storm, he had her married to Ali Quli Beg Istalju entitled Sher Afkun in 1599 when she was 22, which was too advanced an age for the marriage of a girl in medieval times. This shows that her marriage had been, somehow or the other, delayed.

Salim had developed the habit of acquiring and possessing rare, novel and exceptionally beautiful things, which worked wonders on his imagination and he could not forget her. Soon after his accession to the throne in 1605, he engineered the murder of Ali Quli and Mihr-un-Nisa was brought from Burdwan to Agra. He ultimately married her in 1611. Initially, she was given the title: *Nur Mahal* Begum (The Light of the Palace Queen) which was upgraded and, in 1616, she was designated *Nur-Jehan* Begum (The Light of the World Queen). She was an extremely intelligent and crafty woman and an astute calculator. Gradually, she brought the sensuous king under her overdominating influence, and captured and concentrated real political power in her hand. Jehangir was too weak to take any independent decision and the wily lady used him like a puppet. She ruled in his name for eleven years from 1616 to 1627 and became a legend in Mughal history. She sat at the *jharokha* along with the king, and nobles came to pay obeisance to and receive command from, her. *Firmans* were issued and coins were struck in her name. Jehangir so completely surrendered to her that he used to say that she was wise enough to conduct matters of the state and he wanted only six cups of wine and half a *ser* of meat to be contented.

Jehangir was excessively enamoured of her. He used to say that until Nur Jehan came to his house, he had not known domestic pleasure or the spirituality of marriage. This suggests that she was, in fact, an extremely beautiful, healthy and perfect women who could keep such a sensuous man as Jehangir, sexually satisfied. Though a number of drugs and medicines were used in the medieval *harem* to bring out, exhilarate and enhance sexual bliss, it depended no less on the art of sex in which the medieval women were specifically trained in order to win over the lord and to keep him contented to them. This was the greatest weakness of Jehangir and Nur Jehan undoubtedly knew well how to satiate it and to take best advantage from it. She was indeed an accomplished lady of many virtues. She

7. Nur-Jehan's Tomb,Lahore

was dynamic and innovative. She is credited with having invented a large number of dresses, jewellery, perfumes, carpets and ladies' fashions. Her tomb is at Lahore (pl. 7).

(e) Anarkali

More romantic, however, is the legend of Anarkali. Her name was Nadira Begum or Sharf-un-Nisa Begum. She was an excessively beautiful slave-girl in the personal service of Akbar, who had great liking for her and conferred the title *Anarkali* upon her. One day, while seated in an apartment lined with mirrors, he noticed the youthful Anarkali returning Prince Salim (who was just passing by the hall) a smile. Akbar knew the character of his sensuous son more than anybody else, and he was outraged by the suspicion of an affair between the Crown Prince and his own slave-girl. He was so infuriated that he ordered her to be 'built' alive into a wall. Salim could not save her from this cruel end, but after his accession to the throne, he commissioned at Lahore a tomb to her memory. The Persian couplet which he had inscribed on her marble tombstone reads,

Ah! If I could behold the face of

My beloved (*Yar*) once more, I

Would give thanks unto my

God, until the Day of Resurrection.

— Majnun Salim Akbar

(Your Lover Salim, son of Akbar).

This is an expression of passionate love and this testifies that he had really fallen in love with Anarkali. The romance was going on for quite some time. She innocently reciprocated, little knowing the subtle threads of the Mughal polity which bound these human beings called Mughal emperors, and the unfortunate lady paid the price by her life. This also happened in 1599 when Mihr-un-Nisa was married to Sher Afkun and the crown prince was so disappointed and disturbed by the failure of his two romances that he went as far as to rebel against his own father, the mighty Mughal emperor Akbar the Great. The Mughal *harem* was a 'matter of the fact' institution and there was no place for 'romances' in it!

(f) The Lady of the Taj

The *harem* recklessness died with Jehangir. It was cut to size and brought within disciplined and restrained limits by Shah Jehan who, however, did not reduce its glory and glamour, nor did he tamper with its intricate organisation. He married a number of ladies, some of whom have been identified by the contemporary historians, e.g. daughter of Muzaffar Husain Mirza entitled 'Qandahari' Begum; daughter of Shah Nawaz Khan; 'Akbarabadi-Mahal' Begum; 'Sirhindi' Begum and 'Fatehpuri' Begum. He does not seem to have had more than four legal wives at a time and he also did not marry Rajput princesses. Arjumand Bano Begum, grand-daughter of Mirza Ghiyath Beg and niece of Nur Jehan was certainly his chief queen. He married her in 1612 and bestowed upon her the title *Mumtaz Mahal*. She was an exceptionally beautiful lady and he was most affectionately dedicated to her. This attachment was almost exclusive which was a rare phenomenon in a polygamous household. Whenever in the *harem*, he spent most of the time with her and she also always accompanied him on journeys. She bore him fourteen children: eight sons and six daughters (four sons and two daughters survived her) during a brief span of only eighteen years. This ruined her health and it was on the occasion of the birth of her fourteenth child that she died at Burhanpur in 1631. It was to her memory, in order to incarnate her, that the king built the Taj Mahal at Agra (1631-48). (plates 8 to 10).

Aurangzeb tried to simplify the *harem* organisation, though the

8. Taj Mahal, Agra

institution had grown to the dimensions of a banyan tree and it was not possible to undo it. A puritan and devout person, he was not a sex-addict like his grandfather. Names of his queens have been recorded e.g. Dilras Banu, daughter of Shah Nawaz Khan Safawi and mother of Muhammad 'Azam and Muhammad Akbar; Rahmat-un-Nisa entitled Nawab Bai, daughter of Raja Raju of Rajauri and mother of Muhammad Sultan and Muhammad Mua'zzam; Aurangabadi Mahal; Udaipuri Bai (Mahal) mother of Muhammad Kambakhsh; Hira Bai entitled Zainabadi Mahal; Dil-i-Aram; and Daulatabadi Mahal, but, as it appears, he did not have more than four legal wives at a time and, though he also had a number of concubines, he did not indulge in excessive sex. Probably, a mythical spiritual bliss, promised in the Islamic heaven attracted him more than a real sexual bliss. His death in 1707 opened the floodgates of debauchery and licentiousness and

9. Taj Mahal, Agra

10. Taj Mahal, Agra

the later Mughals indulged in a 'free-for-all' situation when the basic norms of dignity and decency were all thrown to the wind, which was certainly blowing towards the decline and doom of the dynasty.

3

Rajput Wives of the Mughals

Right since his accession to the tiny Mughal throne in 1556 A.D., Akbar was tremendously impressed by the loyalty and gallantry of the Rajputs who had a large number of principalities in the adjoining regions of western India. Gradually, he evolved a simple policy. He realised that it was not wise and politically advisable, to alienate them for the sake of some orthodox tenets which, at best, gave little notional satisfaction only. A great empire could be founded in India if they were taken along with it, enrolled as its nobles and made to support it, rather than break it. Their cooperation was the key to his political philosophy. His Rajput policy and *mansabdari* (nobility) system were the outcome of this conviction. While granting them entire freedom in their internal matters, Akbar offered each Rajput raja (prince; chieftain) full protection against external aggression and a *mansab* (military rank) in terms of horses, commensurate to his status, power, prestige and ability. The *mansabdar* was deemed an integral part of the empire. His *mansab* denoted his position in the court and to the world at large, and also ensured a regular monthly income, part of which under the *zat* (personal) rank he kept for himself and the part under *sawar* (horsemen) rank he spent on maintaining the corresponding number of horses. He kept these horses for performing two duties, viz. *chakri* (service) which could be an assignment on a military campaign (*muhim*); and watch and ward duty in the capital (*chowki*). And, of course, he was required to pay personal obeisance to the emperor, acknowledge his sovereignty and pay some annual tribute in token of his submission. *Mansabdari* was, thus, an alliance, vassalage and service—all rolled into one system which constituted the backbone of Akbar's polity. Precisely, a Rajput *mansabdar* was an ally, a vassal and also a noble of the Mughal Empire.

It must be borne in mind that *doli* (literally, bridal palanquin) or the hand of the *mansabdar's* daughter or sister in marriage to the emperor was not a condition of this alliance and Col. James Tod, the political agent of the British East India Co. in Rajputana (1818-22) and those who followed him have erred in interpreting this system as such. Throughout the chronicles, there is no reference to suggest that matrimony was a condition of Akbar's Rajput policy. No marriage was forced upon any raja. It has been shown, on the other hand, that the proposal of marriage always came from the Rajput side. Abu'l Fazl described in detail the circumstances of Akbar's marriage with the daughter of Raja Bharmal of Amer (Ambar or modern Jaipur in Rajasthan), the first of the Rajput princesses married to the Mughals, and showed that the initiative came from the raja and his request was granted by Akbar. The historian again described how Raja Kalyan Mal of Bikaner offered his niece for marriage to Akbar and the latter, 'accepted his proposal'. Similarly, Rawal Har Rai of Jaisalmer took the initiative to propose his daughter's marriage with the emperor who accepted the petition. Abu'l Fazl further noted that Raja Bhagwandas, son of Raja Bharmal of Amer, had a daughter named Manbai, and he wished her to be married to the heir-apparent Prince Salim and his request too was granted. Salim was also similarly married to Jodhbai (who was later entitled *Jagat Gosain*) daughter of Mota Raja Udai Singh of Jodhpur, and then to the daughter of Rai Raisingh of Bikaner.

Abu'l Fazl, Akbar's court historian, discussed the philosophy of marriage in this connection and categorically stated that '...in arranging marriages, they are especially careful about race on both sides, so that there may be good offspring. The effect of putting (good) seed into saline soil illustrates the value of this precaution.' He was equally categorical in his other statement on marriages: 'His Majesty forms matrimonial alliances with princes of Hindustan, and of other countries, and secures by these ties of harmony the peace of the world.' These principles guided the later Mughal marriages too. This shows that the matrimonial relationship with a Rajput raja was intended to cement the alliance and the Mughals certainly sought to derive political advantage out of it. Precisely these were political marriages.

Many aspects of this matter, however, remain obscure and undefined. How the proud Rajputs reconciled with the idea of offering their daughters to Muslims, has not been explained. Was it a political compulsion only? Or were the Mughals, as a martial race admitted in their caste as the kshatriyas? But it was all along one-way traffic and no Mughal princess is recorded to have been married to a Rajput.

Some other important questions also remain to be answered. In the first place, were the Rajput princesses who were married to Akbar and Jehangir converted to Islam on the eve of their marriage as required by the Canon Law? And how were these marriages solemnised, by Hindu or Muslim rites?

Secondly, whether they were allowed to live in their own traditional way, or did they live like Muslim ladies?

Thirdly, were their sons circumcised?

And lastly, were they on death, cremated according to Hindu rites or were their bodies buried in graves according to Islam, tombs having been raised over their remains in any case?

Scholars have generally contended that the Rajput princesses were converted to Islam and the marriage in each case was solemnised according to Islamic law. But what did such a conversion denote? Were these ladies circumcised? Though there is nothing on record in this connection, there is practically no possibility of such a course having been adopted, primarily because female circumcision was not practised by the Mughals. At best, it was formal acceptance of the marriage contract.

That these marriages were performed according to Islam is also doubtful. We do not have full details of the first marriage and all that the court historian had to record is a brief mention that the Raja, '...made the arrangements for the marriage in the most admirable manner and brought his fortunate daughter to this station and placed her among the ladies of the *harem*.' There is absolutely no mention as to how Akbar's various other marriages with the Rajput princesses were solemnised, and every time the historian uses the popular expression that such and such lady was admitted into the imperial *harem*. This is what Badaoni, another historian of Akbar's reign, recorded in respect of Akbar's marriage with the niece of

Raja Kalyanmal of Bikaner: '...she was admitted into the imperial *harem*.' In case of his marriage with the daughter of the prince of Jaisalmer, Akbar even did not go there and Raja Bhagwant Das was sent to bring the lady from there and she: 'obtained eternal glory by entering the female apartments.'

All the three contemporary historians of Akbar recorded the event of Salim's marriage with the daughter of Raja Bhagwandas, son of Raja Bharmal of Amer. Abu'l Fazl made a specific mention of the feasts and assemblies which were held to celebrate this marriage and noted that Akbar: '...and the principal men of the kingdom visited the Rajah's abode and the marriage took place. On the same day the pure form was conveyed to the chamber of fortune and the bridal night of joy was celebrated.'

Nizamuddin, the third historian of Akbar's reign, described this event in greater details and confirmed that the marriage was held in the palace of the Raja: 'in the presence of *qazis* (Islamic judicial officers) and other noble persons.' The presence of *qazis* may or may not allude to their participation in the ceremony and the solemnisation of *nikah* (Muslim marriage) in accordance with the Islamic law, and the reference is, obviously, vague, but Badaoni who was writing his history secretly and had no fear, greed or any other reason to suppress or exaggerate, noted explicitly: '...the Emperor celebrated the ceremony of marriage in the presence of the *qazis* and nobles. And the sum of two *krors* of (silver) *tankahs* (formal currency being a little costlier than rupee) was fixed as the marriage settlement. And they performed all the ceremonies which are customary among the Hindus, such as lighting the fire etc...'.

This shows that though the *mehr* (dower or settlement money) amount was fixed up according to royal customs, the marriage itself was solemnised according to the Hindu rites.

Then, we have absolutely no information about their life in the Mughal *harem* and there are only a few casual and stray allusions, and we do not know how the ladies lived within its precincts. It is difficult to say with any amount of definiteness whether the Rajput ladies, after their marriage, lived in their own way. Some miniature paintings depict *harem* scenes and in them the ladies are shown with *bindi* and bangles, the traditional Hindu feminine ornaments; in a large number of cases they wear tight trousers along with a typical Rajasthani short *choli* (bodice). There is hardly any doubt that they participated in various celebrations in the *harem*, of annual *Nauroz*

11. Temple of Karttikeya, Bengali-Mahal, Agra Fort

(New Year's Day) as well as *tuladan* (weighing ceremony) and regular birthdays.

Badaoni's casual reference may be of some use in this connection:

> From early youth, in compliment to his wives, the daughters of Rajahs of Hind, he had within the female apartments (*harem*) continued to offer the *hom* (fire) which is a ceremony derived from sun worship...

It suggests that the Rajput ladies were free to practise their own religion even within the Mughal *harem.* This is corroborated by a few architectural features remaining in the Bengali Mahal of Agra Fort and the Raniwas at Fatehpur Sikri. A full fledged temple of Karttikeya existed in the former place (pl. 11), while in the latter the western suite has been designed to accommodate a miniature temple (pl. 12). This shows that the Hindu ladies were allowed to live in their own way and follow their own religious and cultural practices, without violating the general norms of the *harem.*

As regards the circumcision of the Mughal princes, we know for certain that, as far as the available data is concerned, the sons and grandsons of Jehangir were not circumcised. (This has been discussed in a following chapter).

Finally, the question remains whether these Rajput princesses married to the Mughals were cremated according to Hindu rites or buried in graves according to Islam. Here too our sources do not help and the available information is too scanty to form a definite opinion. Historians of the reign of Akbar are altogether silent on the death of these ladies. The Kachhwaha princess of Amer, mother

12. Temple in the Raniwas, Fatehpur Sikri

of Jehangir, survived Akbar and had a long tenure of life. She died in Agra in 1623. Jehangir, her own son, mentioned her death very casually: 'On this day 19 Rajab 1032/9 May 1623, news came from Agra that her Highness (Hazrat) Maryam-uz-zamani, by the decree of God, had died. I trust that almighty God will envelop her in the ocean of His Mercy.' It is just a passing reference. There is absolutely no record as to how her last remains were disposed of, or a tomb was built. Her mausoleum, however, very much exists at Sikandara in Agra (pl. 13).

Similarly, Jehangir also casually mentioned, the death of Jodhbai, mother of Khurram (Shah Jehan) at Agra on 30 Rabi' ul-Akhir 1028/5 April 1619:

> On Friday the 30th, the mother of Shah Jehan attained the mercy of God. Next day I myself went to the house of

13. Tomb of Mariam-uz-Zamani, Sikandara, Agra

that precious son and having condoled with him in every way took him with me to the palace. On Sunday, the first Urdibihisht at the auspicious hour chosen by the astrologers and astronomers, I mounted a special elephant of the name of Dilir and in all prosperity and happiness entered the city.

He does not mention whether she was cremated or buried; in fact, he referred to the incident almost formally and on the very third day of the death of his queen, the *Jagat Gosain* or the *Jagat Guru* he entered the capital amidst state rejoicings, without being sincerely aggrieved on his bereavement, as it appears.

Jodhbai's tomb once existed at Agra and, as the record testifies, it was blown up by gunpowder by the British for the sake of its brick and stone which they needed to build barracks.

Jehangir shed some real tears, however, on the death of Khusrau's mother, Manbai, the Kachhwaha princess on whom he had bestowed the title *Shah Begum:*

> His mother, while I was prince, in grief at his (Khusrau's) ways and behaviour and the misconduct of her brother Madhosingh killed herself by swallowing opium (*tiryag*). What shall I write of her excellence and goodness. She had perfect intelligence, and her devotion to me was such that she would have sacrificed a thousand sons and brothers for one hair of mine. She constantly wrote to Khusrau and urged him to be sincere and affectionate to me. When she saw that it was of no use and that it was unknown how far he would be led away, she from the indignation and high spirit which are in Rajput character determined upon death.... At a time when I had gone hunting on Dhil-i-hijja 26th 1013 (May 6, 1605), she in her agitation swallowed a quantity of opium, and quickly passed away. It was as if she had foreseen this behaviour of her unworthy son.
>
> My first marriage and that at the commencement, of my adolescence was with her. After Khusrau's birth, I gave her the title of Shah Begam. When she could not endure the bad conduct of her son and brother towards me she became disgusted with life and died, thereby escaping the present grief and sorrow (owing to Khusrau's recent revolt). In consequence of her death, from the attachment I have for her, I passed some days without any kind of pleasure of life and existence, and for four days, which amount to 32 watches, I took nothing in the shape of food or drink. When

> this tale was told to my revered father (Akbar), a letter of condolence of excessive kindness and affection reached this devoted disciple and he sent me a robe of honour and the auspicious turban tied just as he had taken it off his head.

This shows that Jehangir had special affection for her (he did not have similar feeling for his other queens) and also that he was more humanistic to his ladies as the prince than as the Emperor, who was more an institution than an individual. *That Kingship knows no kinship* was the universal dictum.

Shah Begum's tomb exists at Allahabad (pl. 14) which was Salim's headquarters before accession. It preceded the tombs of other Rajput ladies, e.g. the tomb of Jodhbai and the tomb of Maryam-uz-Zamani. This reinforces the contention that in accordance with

14. Shah Begum's Tomb, Allahabad

the Mughal usage, monumental sepulchres were raised as their memorials. In no case, however, a Rajput lady is buried alongside her husband, in the same tomb. This is puzzling. Were they not duly married wives, or full-fledged Muslims as were of course Asmat Begum and Mumtaz Mahal, who lie buried alongside their husband under the same roof?

The question whether, on death, they were cremated according to Hindu rites or buried according to Islamic law still remains to be answered. Probably, we will have to open some graves to ascertain if they contain full bones or only ashes.

4

Administration of the Mughal Harem

A eunuch[1] was a castrated male employed to serve in women's quarters, viz. *harem*[2] which was a part of the palace set apart for women where no male except the lord of the household was allowed and where women lived in strict seclusion. He was bed-keeper and held the charge of the women.[3] In Muslim *harem*, his was an absolutely confidential position and he exercised important influence. The Mughals were also polygamous and, besides the lawfully married wives, they also kept a large number of concubines and slave-girls in their *harem*. Their *harem*, particularly of Akbar and Jehangir who had, for their personal attendance, service and pleasure, a large number of young and beautiful women from different regions of the Orient, speaking different dialects, all kept in strict seclusion, was an elaborately organised and disciplined institution, with a complex system of officers bearing rigid distinctions of status and function. Abu'l Fazl described the organisation of Akbar's *harem* which, he noted, contained more than five thousand women, each of whom was given a separate apartment.

The security of the *harem* which was a very sensitive matter, 'a vexatious question even for a great statesman' in the words of Abu'l Fazl, was in the hands of faithful and absolutely trustworthy eunuchs.

The officer who was overall incharge (superintendent) of the *harem* quarters was called *nazir* or *Nazir-i-Mahal* or *Nazir-i-Mashkuyah* and under the imperial Mughals, he bore the title of *Khwajasara* (or respected elder, or *Pir* of the household). He was virtually a necessary concommittant of the *harem* and we hear of him through the Persian sources right since the establishment of the Mughal dynasty in India.

Thus, I'tibar Khan Nazir whose name was Khwajah Ambar was a confidential servant of Babur. He also served Humayun. When in 1543, Humayun left Qandahar, I'tibar Khan was placed in charge of the royal ladies. He rendered good service. In A.H. 952/1545 A.D., he waited on Humayun at Kabul and was appointed to serve Akbar. After the death of Humayun, Akbar sent him to Kabul to bring his mother and in the second year of the reign (1557), he accompanied Akbar's mother and other ladies from Kabul to India. After some time, he was made the governor of Delhi and died there.

I'timad Khan was the most important *khwajasara* of the reign of Akbar. His name was Phul Malik. Initially, he served Islam Shah (1545-53) who bestowed upon him the title of Muhammad Khan. On the fall of the Sur empire, he was enrolled among the servants of Akbar, who, after the death of Atagah Khan, appointed I'timad Khan to remodel the finances, granting him a *mansab* (official rank) of 1000 horses and conferring the title, *I'timad Khan* upon him. He served him well and to his satisfaction. In 1565, he conveyed the daughter of Miran Mubarak, King of Khandesh to Akbar's *harem.* Afterwards, he took part in the conquest of Bengal, where he distinguished himself. In 984/1576 he was appointed governor of Bhakkar where he performed with distinction. In 986/1578 when Akbar's presence was required in the Punjab, I'timad Khan desired to join him. In order to equip his contingent, he collected his rents and outstandings with much harshness, which led to a conspiracy against his life and he was murdered, the same year, by one Maqsud

15. Tomb of I'timad-Khan Khwajasara, Itmadpur Agra

'Ali. I'timad Khan founded the suburb of I'timadpur near Agra and built there a large *pucca* tank and other buildings including his own octagonal tomb in the middle of the tank, where he was finally buried (pl. 15).

Several eunuchs have been mentioned during the reign of Jehangir (1605-27). One Said Khan Chaghtai is recorded to have been very fond of eunuchs and he had in his entourage some 1200 good looking and well-trimmed eunuchs. Obviously, these were castrated (emasculated) boys who were customarily made eunuchs in medieval times and sold in the market. Besides rendering various services in the household, these unfortunate souls were also sexually exploited which, though it appears so repugnant to us today, was then a popular practice among the Muslim aristocracy.[4]

Jehangir is recorded to have abolished the custom of castration of boys. Thus he noted in his autobiography:

> In Hindustan, especially in the province of Sylhet which is a dependency of Bengal, it was the custom for the people of those parts to make eunuchs of some of their sons and give them to the governor in place of revenue (*mal-wajibi*). This custom by degrees has been adopted in other provinces and every year some children are thus ruined and cut off from procreation. This practice has become common. At this time I issued an order that hereafter no one should follow this abominable custom, and that the traffic in young eunuchs should be completely done away with. Islam Khan and other governors of the Subah of Bengal received firmans that whoever should commit such acts should be capitally punished, and that they should seize eunuchs of tender years who might be in anyone's possession. No one of the

> former kings had obtained this success. Please, almighty God, in a short time, this objectionable practice will be completely done away with, and the traffic in eunuchs being forbidden, no one shall venture on this unpleasant and unprofitable proceeding.

Khwajah Hilal was also a eunuch. Prior to his entering the service of Jehangir, he was a servant of Qasim Khan Namakin. Runkuta, near Agra, was his *jagir* where he built a small fort and a *serai* and renamed it Hilalabad. He is also recorded to have built a palace near Madar Gate at Agra.

But the most important one, of the reign of Jehangir, bearing the title of *Khwajasara*, was I'tibar Khan Khwajasara. He was a confidante of Jehangir and his attendant from early years. When Khusrau was arrested, he was placed under the charge of I'tibar Khan. The haveli (district surrounding) of Gwalior was placed in the *jagir* of I'tibar Khan probably because Khusrau was imprisoned in the Gwalior Fort. In the fifth year of his reign, in 1610, he got the *mansab* of 4000 *zat* (personal) and 1000 *sawar* (horsemen). This was raised to 5000/2000 in 1613, 5000/3000 in 1615 and 5000/4000 in 1622. Jehangir mentioned him several times in his autobiography and recorded to have received valuable presents from him on several occasions. Thus in 1615, when he was at Ajmer, the offering of I'tibar Khan was placed before him, and what was of the value of 40,000 rupees was accepted. Again, in 1616, while the emperor was still at Ajmer, presents of the value of 56,000 rupees, including a wonderful vessel in the form of a fish jewelled with beautiful gems and a drinking cup calculated to hold his dose of wine, were made for him by I'tibar Khan. In 1622, when he had become very weak and old, the capital Agra with its fort and treasury was placed under his charge, which was, in fact, one of the most important and sensitive posts of the empire. In the eighteenth year of the reign, in 1623, Shah Jehan, who had rebelled against his father, tried to take Agra but I'tibar Khan firmly held out for the Emperor and did not submit. Jehangir was much pleased and recorded that as I'tibar Khan had done approved service in the charge of the Agra Fort, he was dignified with the title of Mumtaz Khan and he gave him the *mansab* of 6000 *zat* and 5000 *sawar*, and having bestowed on him a dress of honour, a jewelled sword, a horse and a special elephant, he sent him back to his duty. I'tibar Khan is recorded to have departed to the other world (i.e. died) at the appointed time, which is a vague reference. It seems that he died soon thereafter, c. 1624. Nothing is, however, known about his family. He built his own tomb in the suburb of Sikandara at Agra, in his lifetime, in accordance with the Mughal custom.

Reference in this connection may also be made to the contemporary Hindi poet Keshavdas who composed his work, *Jehangir-Jas-Chandrika* in praise of Jehangir. It contains verses also in eulogy of the princes as Khusrau and Khurram and a few first-ranking nobles as Mansingh and I'tibar Khan. The verse (*doha*) in praise of I'tibar Khan reads as follows:

Pag ru Patka jarkasi, Bago subh sukumar,

Janat hon I'tibar Khan, Sahi karat itibar. (90).

(His head-dress and waist band are gold embroidered and he wears spotlessly white dress. The king reposes complete trust—*I'tibar*—in him, that is why he is called I'tibar Khan).

This is illustrative of I'tibar Khan's exalted position among the nobles of Jehangir.

The same office of Nazir was held by Firuz Khan Khwajasara under Shah Jehan. He is mentioned in the *Memoirs* (autobiography) of Jehangir in 1619 when a *mansab* of 600 *zat* and 150 *sawar* was conferred upon him. He was at Lahore when Jehangir died (1627). Shahriyar, the wily Nur Jehan's candidate for the throne, hid himself in the *harem* after her manoeuvres failed. Asaf Khan ordered Firzuz Khan Khwajasara to enter the *harem* and bring Shahriyar out. This shows that, normally, he was not allowed to go into the *harem* and it was only at the instance of Asaf Khan, the most powerful person on the spot, that he broke its sanctity. He was promoted to the rank of 2000 *zat* and 500 *sawar* in the first year of Shah Jehan's reign. He held the charge of the palace and has been mentioned in the contemporary histories as *Nazir-i-Mashkuya* (or superintendent of the female apartments) and *Nazir-i-Mahal* in the sense of the custodian or care-taker of the palace.

These representative examples help us to deduce the following facts:

(1) That, originally, eunuchs were necessarily castrated or emasculated men who were employed, customarily, in women's quarter (i.e. *harem*) in the Orient, as the pivot of its organisation.

(2) The Mughals used the title, *Khwajasara* respectfully for the keeper, incharge or superintendent of their *harem*. Precisely, it was the title of the administrative officer of the *harem* who regulated its supplies of stores, salaries and stipends and kept its accounts, fixed duties of the servants and maintained perfect discipline. Whether he was castrated or not, or whether he personally went into the premises of the *harem* is a question.

(3) *Khwajasara*, the superintendent of the *harem* quarters, was an indispensable need of a polygamous household which contained several hundred young and beautiful women, drawn from different linguistic and cultural milieus, kept in strict seclusion exclusively for the pleasure of the king.

(4) As, in medieval times, the palace played a dominant role in state matters, *Khwajasara,* as the presiding officer of the palace, acquired immense influence, power and, as the example of I'tibar Khan shows, wealth.

(5) *Khwajasara* was invariably given handsome *mansabs* even to the extent of 6000/5000, and a high sounding title as *I'timad Khan* and *I'tibar Khan,* like other first-ranking nobles of the court.

(6) It is noteworthy that his title included the suffix *Khan* which denoted his high position in the hierarchy of nobility (Amirs). Could a castrated man, technically a *hijra* (which has obviously a debased social connotation) be called a *Khan* in the Mughal state?

(7) His *harem* duty was not exclusive, and he could be, in fact, he was, transferred from the palace to other important posts and assignments of the state, even to the governorship of the metropolitan towns and the capital. It is simply not possible that the medieval nobility and *ulema*, being what they were temperamentally, could have tolerated a castrated man to rule over them and to occupy such an exalted position in the empire? How, the Mughal emperor himself could have liked to be associated so closely with a eunuch?

(8) *Khwajasara* also commanded sensitive military expeditions and led contingents of Mughals, Afghans and Rajputs. Could this have been possible had he been a eunuch? And would these proud, arrogant and reckless martial races have fought under the command of a *hijra*?

(9) It is also true that absolutely nothing is known about their family and it is doubtful that they married or could marry. This fact amounts to suggest that they were castrated men, probably sexually impotent (and harmless in the context of *harem*) and unable to procreate. But we also do not hear of the families and progenies of some other *mansabdars* and this is not a positive argument. The

fact stands out, predominantly, that they were not only tolerated by the entire state, but were also ungrudgingly obeyed which would not have been possible, in view of the *mizaj* and *tahzib* of the Mughals, had they been eunuchs.

This lead us to conclude, as far as the available data is concerned, that the Mughal *khwajasara*, the *nazir* and administrative officer of the Palace, was not necessarily castrated, and he was as full-fledged a man as other civil and military officers of the empire, and he held the title of *khwajasara* because of his association with the *harem* and not because he was a castrated man himself. The example of Firuz Khan shows that, normally, he was not permitted to go inside the *harem*, a rule which could not have been necessary had he been a eunuch. As the emperor also slept in the *harem* and security of his life was also involved, the privilege of working in this post was extended to an absolutely trustworthy officer in whom total faith could be reposed. Women's apartments contained the most sensitive and inflammatory elements and only an old, tried and thoroughly reliable officer could be entrusted with the job. A man, simply because he was castrated and so was sexually harmless presented no qualification for the post. In fact, such sexually frustrated men, as they naturally tended to be, could be dangerous in the circumstances of a medieval *harem*. Above all is the fact that the *khwajasara* could be transferred to other civil and military departments of the Mughal state like other officers as *vazir* or *diwan* (incharge of finances); *barbegi* (incharge of audiences); *khwansalar* (incharge of kitchen) and *mir-manzil* (incharge of journeys and camps), for example, which shows that he was a full man. *Khwajasara* was therefore, a title which was conferred upon the nazir of the *harem* as a matter of respect and trust which he richly deserved, at least between 1556 and 1658 A.D.

1. From Greek, *Euvouxos, Eunouxos* = one who had charge of a bed; etymologically, one who had charge of women's apartments in Eastern countries; Arabic (*Khasi*) Persian (*Mukhannis*) v. *Hijra* which all denoted a castrated or emasculated human male.

2. Arabic, *Haram* = that which is sacred, e.g. al-Haram, the sacred precincts of Mecca or Madina and also that part of a Muslim household which is set apart for women; it is also used collectively for the women themselves. Hence *huram* = wives. Arabic *harim* is used specifically in Turkey, Egypt and Syria for female apartments of the Muslim household. In Persia, Afghanistan and India, the terms *haramgah, mahal-sarai and zananah* (from Persian, *zan* = women) are also used to denote the same place. Arabic *haram* = forbidden, provides a different etymology.

3. The relationship of the institution of eunuch with *harem* can be traced to most ancient times of human civilisation.

> From remote antiquity among the Orientals as also at a later period in Greece, eunuchs were employed to take charge of the women, or generally as chamberlains. Their confidential position in the *harems* of princes frequently enabled them to exercise an important influence on their royal masters and even to raise themselves to stations of great trust and power. Hence the term eunuch came to be applied in Egypt to any court officer whether a castrate or not. The common idea that eunuchs were necessarily deficient in courage and in intellectual vigour is amply refuted by history. Herodotus states that in Persia they were specifically prized for their fidelity; and they were frequently promoted to the highest offices. The capacity of eunuchs for public affairs is strikingly illustrated by the histories of Persia, India and China and considerable

> power was exercised by the eunuchs under the later Roman emperors. The trade of castrating boys to be sold as eunuchs for Muslim *harems* continued to modern times (*Encyclopaedia Britannica,* vol. viii, p. 814).

It is usual in all parts of the east for wealthy Muslims to keep an establishment of eunuchs to guard the female members of the household, though it is forbidden in the Hadith either to become or to make a 'eunuch'.

4. Thereby also developed the institution of *Saqi*, the 'wine-cup bearer' who was technically a young and handsome 'kept' boy and not a woman, as is generally erroneously supposed. Other sex vices were also prevalent during the medieval times, e.g.
Sodomy – (from the homosexual proclivities of the men of the city of Sodom in ancient Palestine which was destroyed, according to mythology, by God for its wickedness) Carnal copulation with a member of the same sex or with animals; also non-coital, carnal copulation with a member of the opposite sex (coital relates to coitus = natural conveying of semen into the female reproductive tract = vagina). The vice seems to have originated in the desert. There are specific injunctions against this unnatural act, e.g. the *Quran* IV-16. 'If two men among you are guilty of lewdness punish them both.' This shows that it was a pre-Islamic vice of the Arab society which continued unabated like so many other vices, i.e. intoxication, gambling etc. Hence its prohibition in the *Quran*. Sodomy seems to have spread to other countries including India where we have the earliest record in Amir Khusrau's *Mathnawi Shahr-Ashub* otherwise known as *Rubaiyat-Peshawaran* in which were collected the love-quatrains addressed to the artisan boys of Delhi 'in the homosexual sentiment of which the contemporaries found nothing to condemn'. There is absolutely no reference to

sodomy or other similar sex vices in any ancient Indian literature and these were obviously introduced into India during the medieval times.

Other vices such as lesbianism, sadomasochism, sadism, paedophilia and incest were also prevalent.

5

Circumcision among the Muslims

(a) The Rite of Circumcision

Circumcision is removal of the prepuce or foreskin of male and labia-minora (clitoris) of female genitalia. Though many primitive peoples followed this custom, it was essentially a Semitic practice and it was not used by the Aryan races. The custom probably originated in ancient Chaldea and then spread, through the ages, to Egypt on one side and Assyria on the other. It is known to have existed in Egypt in the fourth millennium B.C. The early use of stone knife rather than a metal one suggests the antiquity of the operation.

Among the theories which have been advanced to explain circumcision are that:

1. it is a sacrifice (a substitute for human sacrifice);
2. measure of tolerance of pain;
3. preparation for marriage;
4. consecration of the genitalia;
5. symbolic recognition of the dangers of sexual intercourse;
6. hygienic measure;
7. symbolic castration; and
8. sacrifice or dedication redeeming the male from the God who gave him life.

No single one of these theories is generally accepted. The Hebrews, Egyptians, Muhammedans and various American Indian groups were among those practising it. Many early societies kept it confined to specific class or status groups. It has been estimated that about one-seventh of all males of the world are circumcised.

It is practised as a religious rite by the Jews and Muslims—Islam having borrowed it from Judaism. The circumcision of male Jewish babies on the eighth day represents part of Abraham's Covenant with God and it is obligatory for all male Jews and converts to Judaism. For Jews the relationship with God is a direct and intense one. They believed that God could speak to them through a man like Moses and agreed to accept a code of conduct unique in the ancient world. A mark of their covenant with God (and a substitute for human sacrifice) was the circumcision of every Jew male child. It was, therefore, institutionalised in Judaism.

The Hebrew name for the rite of circumcision as practised by the Jews is B'rith Milah. It is enjoined in the *Book of Genesis* (XVII. 10-14) in which God commands Abraham to circumcise every man-child on the eighth day after birth, and is one of the basic commandments of Judaism. References to the rites are found in the *Bible*.

B'rith Milah is considered a covenant between God and Israel and a symbol of love of the Jew for his people. The rite is performed on the eighth day after birth, no exception made for the Sabbath and holy days, unless postponement is imperative as a health measure. An elaborate ritual takes place on the occasion, the successive steps being called by their Hebrew names Milah, Periah and Metzitzah. The circumciser is called in Hebrew *mohel* and the godfather who holds the child on his lap is called the *sandek*. A chair known as Kisre Shel Eliyahu, or Elijah's Chair (because Elijah in *Malachi*. III. I is called 'messenger of the covenant') also figures in the ceremony.

B'rith Milah is imperative according to Orthodox Jewish law, for a male non-Jew who wishes to convert to Judaism. In Reform Judaism, the matter was controversial during the nineteenth century, but it was determined in 1892 when the Central Conference of American Rabbis voted to dispense with B'rith Milah for proselytes. The Feast of Circumcision, a festival commemorating the circumcision of Jesus is celebrated on January 1 in the Roman Catholic Orthodox and Anglican Churches.

It is noteworthy that though Christ was circumcised, it is not practised by the Christians. The early followers of Christ insisted on circumcision as a pre-requisite for conversion but this was resisted by some potential converts and Paul and Barnabas accepted converts who were not circumcised. After about 50 A.D. pagans could be converted without being circumcised. The early Christian church ruled that its members were not obliged by this Law of Moses (*Acts* 15). Circumcision as a religious rite was abrogated by the Christian law. The *Catholic Dictionary of Theology* (II. 57) held that for a time the rite of circumcision was for a Christian 'dead but not death dealing'; it was in the Pauline sense a dead (worthless) work but did not at once involve its recipient in sin and was in fact carried out upon Timothy by Paul himself (*Acts* 16:3). Exactly when it became a sinful act might be disputed. The church teaches that it is so now, after the promulgation of the Gospel (if done as a religious rite), but in a given situation it might be difficult to say when this promulgation became effective. In missionary lands, the question has been sometimes raised whether circumcision that is practised by pagans as a rite of puberty should be tolerated.

From the medical point of view, the operation of removing the foreskin to allow its free retraction beyond the glans-penis prevents the accumulation, from a number of glands, of an odoriferous cheese like substance called smegma which can cause discomfort besides being unhygienic. It has been observed that the Hindus who do not practise circumcision suffer far more frequently from cancer of penis than the Muslims who circumcise ritually. Among the Jews, cancer of penis virtually never occurs. The operation of circumcision is routinely performed on the newborn as a hygienic procedure in some parts of the western world.

Scholars have discussed the medical aspect of this matter in full details. It is generally believed that phimosis, which is a source of many diseases of male organ, is usually caused due to congenital narrowing of the preputial orifice, often associated with an unduly long foreskin. The condition can be acquired as a result of chronic or acute inflammation of the lining of the prepuce which invariably is accompanied by some degree of inflammation of the glands. If the foreskin cannot be retracted, smegma accumulates beneath it and some degree of balanoposthitis results. In extreme examples of congenital phimosis, when the patient micturates, the prepuce baloons out first and a fine, weak stream of urine follows. Dysuria with residual urine hydro-ureters, and hydro-nephoroses are rarely due to phimosis, but more often occurs as a result of arresiameati which may be hidden by the phimosis. Minor degree of the phimosis in early infancy can be treated by regular retraction of the prepuce, but in other circumstances, circumcision is inevitable. Paraphimosis is another disease of similar kind which is caused as a result of tight prepuces. In circumcised people this does not appear. The most dangerous disease of the male organ is penile cancer, which is practically unknown amongst circumcised Jews and is uncommon among Muslims who are circumcised before puberty. Penile harper is another disease which is due to a virus infection. It occurs frequently on the glands and the prepuce. It also hardly arises among the circumcised people.

It is a Semitic practice and it is quite likely that it originated in desert or arid regions where water was scarce, circumcision ensured greater cleanliness. In the regions where sodomy was practised, it ensured better cleanliness. Its usefulness later led the society to give it the form of a religious rite.

Female circumcision or excision is widely practised in such places as New Guinea, Australia, the Malay archipelago, Ethiopia, Egypt and other parts of Africa, southern Europe and South America and by various Islamic peoples of western Asia and India. The operation consists in cutting away the whole or part of the external genitalia. It is quite possible that female circumcision antedates male circumcision. However, there is hardly any consideration of cleanliness in female circumcision.

Another aspect which seems to have contributed in a larger degree to the popularity and sanctification of male circumcision is the sexual advantage which accompanies it. The removal of the foreskin from the glans gradually hardens it, reducing its sensitivity and tremendously enhancing retention during copulation and the consequential sexual pleasure to both the participants, and the mutual sentimentality which depends, essentially, on the biology of sex. Circumcision is reported, in fact, to enhance potential male sexuality and to heighten the sexual life of the couple.

Islam like Christianity drew largely on Judaism and it borrowed circumcision also from this source. Arabic word for circumcision is *khitan, khitanah* or *khatnah.* Surprisingly, circumcision is not even once mentioned in the *Quran* though it is one of the very basic customs of orthodox Islam. It is held to be founded upon the traditions of the Prophet and the institution is said to have dated from the time of Abraham. In fact many customs and institutions of *Jahiliyah* period were retained by the Prophet and circumcision is one of them. It is the *sunnah* of the prophet and not the divine order. However, as *sunnah* is also necessary for the Muslims, so circumcision is also binding on them. There are different views on its legal aspect. According to Ahmad b. Hanbal, it is a compulsory '*sunnah*', whereas Imam Shafi'i considers it *rahab.* By and large, *Khatna* is called *Sunnat ul-Rasul;* it is *tariqa* (way of life), not a *farz* (basic duty). Some writers hold the view that Muhammad was born circumcised (*muna-khatnah*), though this is not generally accepted. Three traditions related to circumcision are recorded in the *Sahihu'l-Bukhari* which show that the practice was gradually accepted and incorporated in Islam.

The Prophet had to reckon tremendously with Jewish people and culture during the formative period of his religion. Originally, he tried his best to make a compromise with the Jews and adopted some conciliatory measures, e.g. the making of Jerusalem as the universal *Qiblah* of Islam. But the Jews did not respond favourably. On being disappointed, he decided to stop all overtures and changed the *Qiblah* to Mecca (*Quran*, II. 144) in 624 A.D. Infact, the three religions: Judaism, Christianity and Islam drew on a common mythology and the beliefs and practices of the earliest of them, viz. Judaism was a source for the two later creeds and it was from the same source that they learnt the custom of circumcision. While Christianity ultimately abrogated it, it became an essential socio-religious rite under Islam.

It is compulsory for all male Muslim children and converts to Islam to be circumcised. Female circumcision is also practised in Arabia though it is unknown in India where male circumcision is referred to as *sunnat* (the quality of one's being a follower of Islam). Though there is no fixed age, and it may be performed at 6 days or 4 years or 10 years. Customarily its operation is performed in India after the child is four years of age, and a barber conversant with the practice is employed to do it. A bit of stick is used as a probe, and carried round and round between the glans and prepuce, to ascertain the exact extent of the fraenum, and that no unnatural adhesions exist. The foreskin is then drawn forwards and a pair of forceps, consisting of a couple of pieces of split bamboo, five or six inches long and a quarter of an inch thick, tied firmly together at one end with a string to the extent of an inch, applied from above in an oblique direction so as to exclude about an inch and a half of the prepuce above and three-quarters of an inch below. The forceps severely grasping it, causes a good deal of pain but this state of suffering does not continue long, since the next thing to be done is the removal which is done by one stroke of the razor drawn directly downwards. The haemorrhage which follows is inconsiderable and easily stopped by the application of burnt rags and ashes.

According to some Muslim jurists, seventeen prophets, viz. Zakariya, Shis, Idris, Yusuf, Hanzalah, Isa, Musa, Adam, Nuh, Shu'aib, Sam, Lut, Salih, Sulaiman, Yahya, Hud and Muhammad were born circumcised. This statement traditionally records the great antiquity of the practice of circumcision in the Semitic middle-east where the three world religions were born.

(b) Discontinuity of circumcision by the Mughals

Male circumcision was practised by Muslims as an article of their faith (*Sunnat'ul-Rasul*) and as a religious rite, all over the world. The Chaghtais (Mughals) also practised it. Babur writing about his father Umar Sheikh Mirza noted that his father first gave him Kabul and, with Baba-i-Kabuli for his guardian, had allowed him to set out, but recalled him from the Tamarik valley to Samarqand on account of the Mirza's circumcision feast. While narrating the affairs of Sultan Husain Mirza over the possession of Balkh and Astarabad (1496-97 A.D.), he again recorded that: 'Ali Sher Beg had gone but Badi-uz-Zaman Mirza would not consent to give up Astarabad and he said, "The Mirza assigned it to my son Muhammad Mu'min Mirza at the time of his circumcision".' These records show that circumcision was an important occasion and a circumcision-feast was a regular feature of the Mirza (Chaghtai; later called Mughal) household, life and culture, right since the time of Babur.

Humayun was born on Ah. 4 *Dhil-q'ad* 913/6 March 1508 A.D. in the citadel of Kabul. His circumcision customarily fell due in 1512. But there is a break in the narrative of the *Baburnamah* from 914/1508 to 925/1519, i.e. for about eleven years which remain as unchronicled years. Hence no reference to Humayun's circumcision which, in any case, should have been performed and celebrated as a regular custom.

Akbar was born on 5 Rajab 949/15 October 1542. Gulbadan

Begum recorded the event of his circumcision as follows:

> A few days later, he (Humayun) sent persons to bring Hamida Banu Begum from Qandahar. When she arrived, they celebrated the feast of the circumcision of the Emperor Jalalu'd-Din Muhammad Akbar. Preparations were made and after the new year, they kept splendid festivity for seventeen days. People dressed in green and thirty and forty girls were ordered to wear green and come out to the hills. On the first day of the New Year, they went out to the Hill of Seven Brothers and there passed many days in ease and enjoyment and happiness. The Emperor Muhammad Akbar was five years old when they made the circumcision feast in Kabul. They gave it in the same large Audience Hall Garden. They decorated all the *bazars*. Mirza Hindal and Mirza Yadgar Nasir and the Sultans and Amirs decorated their quarters beautifully and in Bega Begam's garden, the begams and ladies made theirs quite wonderful in a new fashion.

That Akbar was circumcised and the occasion was celebrated has been confirmed by Khwajah Nizamuddin Ahmed (952/November 1545). He noted that, 'great entertainments were arranged at this time (after Humayun's entry into Kabul) and the ceremony of circumcision of His Highness the Prince was celebrated…'

It is Sheikh Abu'l Fazl, the court historian, finally, who gives a detailed description of the event in the *Akbarnamah* under a separate heading: 'Celebration of the Shahinshah's Circumcision'. The ceremony was performed in the Urta-Bagh and the celebration lasted several days. Each day, there was a novel royal feast and

Humayun distributed generous gifts; '...the circumcision of His Majesty the Shahinshah was held with thousands of rejoicings... the captains presented their gifts, and were exalted by grand favours...(Humayun) bade preparations be made for a great feast. He distributed fiefs, presents and robes of honour to the servants of the threshold in accordance with their deserts.'

Humayun captured Kabul from Kamran on 18 November 1545 and Akbar's circumcision ceremony was held soon thereafter, possibly in November 1545 itself.

Prince Salim (later named Jehangir) was born at Fatehpur Sikri on 17 Rabi'ul-Awwal 977/30 August 1569. He and his younger brothers Murad and Daniyal were circumcised and all the three major historians of the age have recorded the event. Thus, Badaoni noted on the 25th of this month, the rite of circumcision was performed on their Imperial highnesses, the Emperor's sons. Nizamuddin also recorded that when Akbar was at Fatehpur Sikri: 'the circumcision of the fortunate princes was ordered and magnificent festivities were arranged.' The ceremony was held on 20 Jamadi'ul-Akhir 981/22 October 1573 when Salim was four years one month and twenty-two days old, Murad was 3-4-15 and Daniyal was only 1-1-13 (according to the solar calendar).

Abu'l Fazl discussed the rationale of circumcision and his record of this event is most important:

> One of the occurrences was the festival for the circumcision of the glorious princes. In as much as the keeping alive of old customs is a strong pillar of administration, and the following in the steps of predecessors is an essential point in the management of the external world, and especially as the wearers of scarves and turbans (i.e. Ulema) regard

> Use and Wont as related to the Divine laws, and most of all because rulers search for opportunities for feasts and make them an occasion for liberality and forgiveness, His Majesty determined upon celebrating the circumcision of the princes.

This is very illustrative. Thus, he cited three reasons which induced Akbar to follow this practice, though Abu'l Fazl's narrative implies that he (Akbar) did not like it, like other things related to the orthodox religion of Islam, including the Arabic language—the practice of which he discontinued. The three compulsions the court historian alluded to were the need and expediency:

a. to follow old customs which reinforced the credibility of a state;

b. to keep the *Ulema* in good humour by adhering to some of the fundamental tenets of Islam and thus maintaining a status quo; and

c. to organise functions and ceremonies with regal display to impress upon the people the might and grandeur of the empire.

Abu'l Fazl's narrative suggests, however, that Akbar was following the custom reluctantly and with constraint.

These contemporary records, in any case, show, unequivocally, that:

1. Circumcision was performed on the Mughal princes at least upon prince Salim (Jehangir);

2. The occasion was celebrated in royal fashion; and
3. The event was recorded by contemporary historians without fail.

The third point is the most important. This shows that it was not a private affair of the *harem*, but a great public ceremony which was organised by the state and that it was not less important than *Nauroz*, *Tuladan* or birthday ceremonies. Circumcision celebrations were invariably recorded both by official and non-official chroniclers as an historically important event. This is significant.

It is quite unusual, therefore, that in the third generation from Akbar, we have no record of the circumcision of Mughal princes. For example, Khusrau and Khurram (Shah Jehan), sons of prince Salim (Jehangir) were born on 24 Amardad 995/ 6 August 1587 and 30 Rabi'ul-Awwal 1000/ 5 January 1592 respectively, both at Lahore. Their circumcision customarily fell due in 1591 and 1596 respectively, during the lifetime of Akbar himself. But there is absolutely no mention of, or even a casual allusion to their circumcision in the contemporary histories of Abu'l Fazl, Nizamuddin and Badaoni, nor does their father Jehangir refer to their circumcision in his *Memoirs*. Why, when *Naurozs, Tuladans* and birthdays were meticulously recorded simultaneously, did these historians fail to record their circumcision which was an important event of the Mughal state since the time of Babur?

In the circumstances which are distinctly before us, this could have been possible owing to one factor only, that the circumcision of these princes was not done at all and the contemporary historians had nothing to record. Looking at the fact that Akbar followed this custom very reluctantly in 1573 when Prince Salim was circumcised, as discussed above, it seems quite possible and even probable that, as soon as he found himself absolutely secure in his position, and he could venture to initiate his own innovations (as is reflected by his institutions of *Ibadat-Khanah* (1576), *Mahzar* (1579), *Allopanisad* (1580), *Din-i-ilahi* (1582), *Tarikh-i-ilahi* (1584), *Surya-Darsana, Tuladan* and *Jharokha-Darsana*) he discontinued the practice of circumcision of the Mughal princes. This inference is supported by the circumstances which followed the institution of *Ibadat-Khanah* at Fatehpur Sikri (1576 A.D.). Thus, Badaoni, an eye-witness, noted:

> His Majesty had also the early history of Islam read out to him, and soon began to think less of the Sahabah (Companions and followers of the prophet Muhammad). Soon after, the observance of the five prayers (Namaz) and the fasts (Roza) and the belief in everything connected with the prophet, were put down as vain superstitions, and man's reason, not tradition, was acknowledged as the only basis of religion. Portuguese priests also came frequently, and His Majesty enquired into the articles of their belief which are based upon reason.

This contains an allusion to the discontinuance of several Islamic practices which could have included circumcision. It may be noted that Roman Catholic priests have also been referred to in Badaoni's note. Circumcision is primarily a Jewish custom (*The Book of Genesis,* XVII. 10-14) and, as a religious rite, it was abrogated by the Christian law. The Christian fathers could have reinforced Akbar's disbelief in and disapproval of the practice of circumcision and it was finally stopped.

Badaoni referred to Akbar's rejection of Islamic beliefs: 'And the Resurrection and Judgement, and other details and traditions of which the prophet was the repository, he laid all aside.'

He was gradually inclined towards Hinduism:

> On hearing further how much the people of the country prized their institutions, he began to look upon them with affection…and having instituted research into doctrines of the sects of Hindu unbelievers, …he took so much pleasure in such discussions that not a day passed but a new fruit of this loathsome tree ripened into existence. (Al-Badaoni, *Muntakhabu't-Tawarikh*, vol. II, trans. W.H. Lowe p. 265)

The Roman Catholic padres were invited from Goa and they had disputations in the *Ibadat-Khanah.* Badaoni noted that his majesty firmly believed in the truth of the Christian religion and wishing to spread the doctrines of Jesus, ordered Prince Murad to take a few lessons in Christianity under good auspices, and charged Abu'l Fazl to translate the Gospel. Instead of the usual *Bismillah'ir-Rehman-ir-Rahim* the following line was used, *Ai Nami vay Gesu Christu* (praise be upon Jesus Christ).

These proceedings impressed upon Akbar the utter futility of the orthodox point of view and the worthlessness of some Islamic practices which had originated in the desert conditions of Arabia.

Abu'l Fazl recorded the net result in the words of Akbar himself as follows:

> Most persons, from intimacy with those who adorn their outside, but are inwardly bad, think that outward semblance,

> and the letter of Muhammedanism, profit without internal conviction. Hence, we by fear and force compelled many believers in the Brahman (i.e. Hindu) religion to adopt the faith of our ancestors. Now that the light of truth has taken possession of our soul, it has become clear that on this distressful place of contrarities, where darkness of comprehension and conceit are heaped up, fold upon fold, a single step cannot be taken without the torch of proof, and that, that creed is profitable which is adopted with the approval of wisdom. To repeat the Creed (viz. the Kalma), to remove a piece of skin (i.e. *Khatna*, circumcision) and to place the end of one's bone on the ground (i.e. *Sijdah*) from the dread of Sultan, is not seeking after God.

This is an extremely important reference. Thus, Abu'l Fazl made a record of Akbar's total disapproval of such basic things of Islam as *Kalma*, *Khatnah* (circumcision) and *Namaz*. We know for certain that he changed *Kalma* to read *Allo-Rasul Mahamad Akbarasya Allo-Allam ilalleti-illallah* and instead of showing veneration to the Ka'aba he worshipped the sun publicly. His disapproval of circumcision has also been explicitly recorded and, quite likely, like his other revolutionary measures, he could have stopped this practice, probably after 1585 A.D. when he was fully secure politically and firmly in command of the things. It may be owing to this reason that the sons of prince Salim, born thereafter, were not circumcised and, hence, no record of such a ceremony is available in any contemporary work. If they had been circumcised, the occasion in each case should have been celebrated in royal fashion and duly recorded in the chronicles.

The following table shows the record of circumcision of the Mughal princes (from Akbar to Aurangzeb):

	Date of birth	*Date of circumcision and its celebration*
I. Akbar	5 Rajab 949/15 October 1542 at Amarkot	Ramadhan 952/ November 1545 at Kabul
II. Salim (Jehangir)	17 Rabi'ul-Awwal 977/30 August 1569 at Fatehpur Sikri.	20 Jamadi'ul-Akhir 981/22 October 1573 at Fatehpur Sikri.
III. (1) Khusrau	24 Amardad 995/6 August 1587 at Lahore	No record
(2) Khurram (Shah Jehan)	30 Rabi'ul-Awwal 1000/5 January 1592 at Lahore	No record
IV. (1) Dara	29 Safar 1024/20 March 1615 at Ajmer	No record
(2) Aurangzeb	15 Dhil-q'ad 1027/24 October 1618 at Dohad	No record

There is another reference which reinforces this contention.

In his *Memoirs* of the year 1611, Jehangir recorded an order to the Amirs of the distant provinces, not to sit in the *jharokha*, or to have elephant-fights, or to cut off ears and noses, or to force Islam on any one (*Taklif-i-Musalmani bar kasi nakunand*). *Taklif-i-Musalmani,* obviously, refers to the pain which accompanies the Muslim ceremony of circumcision and this reference is to the same. That is why, injunction comes in immediately after the prohibition against blinding and mutilation. This seems to be a reiteration of the general order prohibiting circumcision in the empire which was, in fact, a continuation of Akbar's policies, institutions and principles which Jehangir faithfully followed to the extent that though he knew he was not a *guru* of Akbar's stature, he continued to initiate *chelas* of the *Din-i-ilahi*.

It transpires, therefore, that the practice of circumcision had been stopped by Akbar and Jehangir adhered to this prohibition, and hence the Mughal princes were not circumcised. Dara and Aurangzeb, in the fourth generation from Akbar, for example, were born on 29 Safar 1024/20 March 1615 at Ajmer and 15 *Dhil-q'ad* 1027/24 October 1618 at Dohad respectively, but no contemporary chronicler has recorded ceremony of their circumcision which, in all probability, was not performed; otherwise the historians had no reason to omit it from their records. Even Jehangir does not mention the event in his *Memoirs*.

That their children would not be circumcised was never a condition of Mughal matrimonies with Rajput princesses. The reason could be different. Circumcision was a Semitic rite and the Hindus did not practice it. The Mughals abandoned its practice to be more akin to Indian environment, so as to be more acceptable to the people of India, whose paramount (*Cakravartin*) king they professed to be. It was a bold step to shed pretensions to pan-Arabic Islamic faiths and beliefs to be more homogeneous and integral to the land, the people and culture of India.

6
Mughal Kitchen, Dining Etiquette & Cuisine

The Mughal kitchen was an institution in itself, of which every detail was precisely worked out, regulated and recorded. The ladies of the *harem* did not cook their meals. There was a common kitchen attached to the precincts of the *harem*, though adequately separated from it in order to maintain seclusion and *purdah*. Expert cooks were engaged in it. It supplied all food-requirements of the *harem* inmates. No cooking was allowed inside the *harem* and the Rajput ladies married to the Mughals also ate from the common kitchen.

(a) Management of the Kitchen

It was, in fact a full-fledged independent department. Trustworthy experienced persons specialised in various matters of the kitchen were appointed to this department. Enough funds and servants were allocated to it. Its head was called *Mir-Bakawal.* Sometimes he was also called *Khwansalar* (Incharge of the Kitchen). He was assisted by *Vazir* (Prime Minister) himself who was specifically entrusted to see that it functioned well and properly. Such was the sensitive nature of the kitchen that the King himself kept a vigilant watch on its working. Only an extremely honest, trusted, intelligent and experienced officer was appointed *Mir-Bakawal* (Master or Head of the Imperial kitchen). He was assisted by several competent officers called *Bakawals* (Supervisors of the Kitchen). There were separate treasuries for cash and stores (*kothiyar* or *bhandar*). Several tasters and a clever writer were attached to this department. Cooks specialised in various vegetarian and non-vegetarian dishes were requisitioned from all regions and countries. They prepared a great variety of dishes of all kinds of grains, greens and meats; dry and oily; and sweet (*mitha*) and spicy *(chatpata*). That 52 types of dishes were prepared only from *chana* (gram) and *besan* (flour of gram-pulse) gives an idea of the variety of dishes.

Such dishes were prepared every day. Though Akbar ate only once in 24 hours, as his historian has recorded, and he left off before he was fully satisfied, his successors loved to eat good food, both exquisitely and sumptuously. It is noteworthy that there was no fixed time for a meal. Dishes were continuously in preparation and the servants had the things always so far ready that in the space of an hour after the order had been given, a hundred dishes could be served up. The food allowed to the women of the seraglio was taken from the kitchen from morning till night, and the Mughal kitchen worked almost round the clock.

The affairs of the kitchen were meticulously managed. In the beginning of the year, the sub-treasurers or clerks of the kitchen made out an annual estimate and received the amount. The money bags and the door of the store house were sealed with the seals of the *Mir-Bakawal* and the writer. Every month, a correct statement of the daily expenditure of the kitchen was drawn up, the receipt for which was sealed by the same two officers, when it was entered under the head of the expenditure. Its was thus a very systematised working and everything was recorded in black and white. At the beginning of every quarter, the *Diwan-i-Buyutat* (The Superintendent of Stores and Workshops) and the *Mir-Bakawal* requisitioned the necessary stores for the kitchen, e.g. *Sukhdas* rice from Bahraich; *Dewzira* rice from Gwalior; *Jinjin* rice from Rajauri and Nimlah; *Ghee* (Clarified Butter) from Hisar Firoza etc. Other things were readily available locally and the *banjara* (roving traders of grain) were engaged to maintain a constant supply of foodgrains when the king and his *harem* were on a journey and lived in camp. Livestock of *qaz* (goose), water-fowls and certain vegetables were obtained from Kashmir. Sheep, goats, berbery goats, fowls, *qaz* and other birds and animals, whose flesh was greatly relished, were luxuriously fed and fattened by the cooks. These were maintained so as to provide fresh and healthy meat for cooking.

The slaughter-house of the imperial kitchen was established securely outside the city or the camp, near a river or tank, so that the meat could be adequately washed. After washing, it was sent to the kitchen in sacks sealed by the cooks. It was again washed in the kitchen and thrown into the cooking pots, under the watchful eyes of the supervisors. The *bhishtis* (water-carriers) poured water out of their leather bags into earthen vassels (*ghadas* or *ghata*), the mouths of which were covered with pieces of cloth and sealed up. This water was left to settle before it was used for cooking. A kitchen-garden was also maintained for the continuous supply of fresh green vegetables.

The *Mir-Bakawal* and the writer periodically determined the price of every eatable which became a fixed rule for the term. The following were the prices of some articles used in the Mughal kitchen in Akbar's age (c. 1600 A.D.):*

Grains & Pulses

Gehun (wheat)	-	12 *dam* per *man*
Kabulichana (*Kabul-gram*)	-	16
Kalachana (black gram)	-	8
Masuri (lentil)	-	12
Jaw (barley)	-	8
Jwar (barley)	-	10
Bajra (millet)	-	6
Alsi (linseed)	-	10
Mushang (peas)	-	6
Sarson (mustard seed)	-	12
Mushkin Dhan (paddy)	-	110
Sada Dhan (paddy)	-	100
Sukhdas rice	-	100
Dunaprasad rice	-	90
Samzira rice	-	90
Shakarchini rice	-	90
Dewzira rice	-	90
Jinjin rice	-	80

* Table of currency and weights have been given at the end of this chapter.

Zirhi rice	-	40 *dam* per *man*
Sathi rice	-	20
Mung Sabut (kidney bean)	-	18
Mash (a pulse)	-	16
Moth (a pulse)	-	12
Lobiya (a bean)	-	12
Mung dal	-	18
Kodon	-	7
Masuri dal	-	16
Moth dal	-	12
Wheat flour (Fine)	-	22
Wheat flour (Coarse)	-	15
Barley flour	-	11

Vegetables

Soyasag (fennel)	-	10 *dam* per *man*
Palak (spinach)	-	16
Pudina (mint)	-	40
Pyaz (onion)	-	6
Lahsun (garlic)	-	40
Shaljam (turnip)	-	21
Bandgobhi (cabbage)	-	1 *dam* per *ser*
Dunwretu	-	2
Shaqaqul (wild carrot)	-	3
Garlic flowers	-	1
Jitu	-	3

Adrakh (ginger)	-	2½ *dam* per *ser*
Kachnar buds	-	½
Chuka	-	½
Bathuwa	-	¼
Ratsaka	-	1

Note: Surprisingly *Alu* (potato), the king of modern vegetables has not been mentioned in the medieval lists. Nor is there *Tamatar* (tomato).

Livestock & Meat

Dashmandi sheep	-	6½ *rupiya* per head
Afghan sheep (1st kind)	-	2
Afghan sheep (2nd kind)	-	1½
Afghan sheep (3rd kind)	-	1¼
Kashmir sheep	-	1½
Hindustani sheep	-	1½
Barbari goat (1st kind)	-	1
Barbari goat (2nd kind)	-	¾
Qaz (goose)	-	20 *dam* per head
Battakh (duck)	-	1 *rupiya* per head
Tughdari (bustard)	-	20 *dam* per head
Kulang (crane)	-	20
Jarz (abustard)	-	18
Durraj (black partridge)	-	3
Kabg (partridge)	-	20
Budana	-	1

Lawah	-	1 *dam* per head
Karwanak (stone curlew)	-	20
Fakhta (dove)	-	4
Mutton (sheep)	-	65 *dam* per *man*
Mutton (goat)	-	54

Butter & Sugar etc.

Ghee (clarified butter)	-	105 *dam* per *man*
Oil (mustard)	-	80
Milk	-	25
Curd	-	18
Khand (refined sugar)	-	6 *dam* per *ser*
Mishri (sugarcandy)	-	5½
Tagar (white sugar)	-	128 *dam* per *man*
Bura (brown sugar)	-	56

Spices

Zafran (*Keshar*; saffron)	-	400 *dam* per *ser*
Lavang (*Laung;* clove)	-	60
Ilaychi (cardamom)	-	52
Kali Mirch (round pepper)	-	17
Pipal (long pepper)	-	16
Sonth (dry ginger)	-	4
Adarakh (ginger)	-	2½
Zira (cuminseed)	-	2
Saunf (aniseed)	-	2

Haldi (turmeric)	-	10 *dam* per *ser*
Dhaniya (coriander seed)	-	3
Kalaunji (siyahdana)	-	1½
Hing (asafoetida)	-	2 *dam* per *tola*
Dalchini (cinnamon)	-	40 *dam* per *ser*
Namak (salt)	-	16 *dam* per *man*

Note: Surprisingly, *Lal-Mirch* (red chillies) has not been mentioned in this list. It may also be noted that most of these are classical indigenous spices which had been in use in India since ancient times. Some of these are, in fact, Ayurvedic medicines which have been permanently admitted into the Indian kitchen.

Pickles (*Achar*)

Achar Nibu (lime)	-	6 *dam* per *ser*
Nibu Ras (plain lemon juice)	-	5
Sirka (vinegar)	-	5
Ganna-Sirka (sugarcane vinegar)	-	1
Achar Ashtarghar	-	8
Achar Am (mango in oil)	-	2
Achar Am (mango in vinegar)	-	2
Achar Nibu (lemon in oil)	-	2
Achar Nibu (lemon in vinegar)	-	2
Achar Nibu (lemon dry in salt)	-	1½
Achar Nibu (lemon in lemon-juice, i.e. *nibu-ras*)	-	3
Achar Adrakh (ginger)	-	2½

Achar Adarshakh	-	2½ *dam* per *ser*
Achar Shaljam (turnips in vinegar)	-	1
Achar Gajar (carrot)	-	½
Achar Bans (bamboo)	-	4
Achar Seb (apple)	-	8
Achar Lahsun (garlic)	-	1
Achar Pyaz (onion)	-	½
Achar Kishmish-Munaqqa (raisins)	-	8
Achar Kachnar	-	2
Achar Shaftalu (peach)	-	1
Achar Sahajna (horse radish)	-	1
Achar Karil-buds (capparis)	-	½
Achar Tenti (Karil berries)	-	½
Achar Sarson (mustard)	-	¼
Achar Turai	-	½
Achar Kakadi-Khira (cucumber)	-	½
Achar Badrang (gourd)	-	½
Achar Kachalu	-	½
Achar Muli (radish)	-	½

Note: That pickles (*achar*) of bamboo, apple and raisins were also prepared and available in the market during the medieval times is noteworthy.

The *Mir-Bakawal* and the writer signed the day-book, the estimates, the receipts for transfers, the list of wages of the servants and maintained a record of everything. They watched and controlled every transaction. Bad characters, idle-talkers and unknown persons were never employed. No one was entertained without a personal security and reliable reference. Acquaintance only was not sufficient.

(b) System of Service

Service of the dishes was also a thoroughly systematic affair. The victuals were served up in dishes of gold and silver, bowls of *pai-zahar* and other semi-precious stones, and earthenware. *Pai-zahar* was a variety of *zahar-mohra,* roughly from the jade (*Yashab*) family, of light green or greenish yellow colour. It was an antidote of poison and crockery of this stone was mostly used in the imperial dining, by way of precaution. Dishes were prepared and served under each of the *Naib-Bakawals.* During the time of cooking and when the bowls and dishes were taken out, a *chandova* (awning) was spread and onlookers kept away. The cooks tucked up their sleeves and the hems of their garments and held their hands before their mouths and noses when the food was taken out. The respective cook and the *bakawal* tasted it, after which it was tasted by the *Mir-Bakawal* and put into the dishes. The gold and silver dishes were tied up in red clothes, and those of copper and china in white ones. The *Mir-Bakawal* attached his seal and wrote on it the names of the contents, whilst the clerk of the pantry wrote out on a sheet of paper a list of all vessels and dishes which were sent inside, with the seal of the *Mir-Bakawal,* so that none of the dishes could be changed. The dishes were carried by the *bakawals,* the cooks and other servants, and mace-bearers preceding and following, to prevent people from approaching them. The servants of the pantry also sent in bags containing the seal of the *bakawal,* various kinds of bread, saucers of curds piled up and small stands containing plates of pickles, fresh ginger, limes and various green vegetables. The king dined in the *harem*. The servants of the palace again tasted the food, spread the table-cloth (*dastar-khwan*), on the floor over the carpet and arranged the dishes. When the king began to dine, the table servants sat opposite him in attendance. First, the share of the *derwishes* (recluses) was put apart. The king began with milk or curd. After he had dined, he prostrated himself in prayer. The *Mir-Bakawal* was constantly in attendance when the king dined. Akbar did not dine with the ladies of the *harem* who were free to eat in their respective quarters. *Harem* inmates dined together only on festive occasions, when the king also joined them.

This precaution was absolutely necessary in medieval times. The Mughals remembered only too well that their ancestor Babur was poisoned, in Hindustan, by a cook bribed by the mother of Ibrahim Lodi who was defeated and killed by him in the battle of Panipat in 1526. Though it was immediately detected and he vomited, ultimately he died by the effect of the indigenous concoction of the deadly poison *kalakuta* which was administered to him. Fear of being poisoned in such a vast establishment as this was real and this system of precise checks and controls was evolved to rule out this possibility. The Mughals followed this system practically as far as the middle of the 18th century A.D., whereafter they could not afford it.

An English lady who lived in the *harem* of a noble in the early 19th century has left an eye-witness description of the ladies' dinner, which had assumed the status of an etiquette (*tahzib*). She noted that they did not use tables or chairs and dined on the floor. It was first matted with coarse date-leaf matting (called *chatai*), over which *shatranjis* or *durries* (thick cotton carpets) were spread. A white calico carpet or *chadar* (sheet) covered the *shatranji*. A *dastarkhwan* (table-cloth) was spread on the *chadar*. They did not use knives, forks, spoons, glasses or napkins 'so essential to the comfortable enjoyment of a meal amongst Europeans. But those who never knew such comforts had to desire for the indulgence, nor taste to appreciate them.' (*Observations on the Musalmans of India*, vol. I, p. 304, Mrs. Meer Ali)

The dinner was brought into the *zenanah* in native earthenware, on trays. As they did not use spoons or forks, there was no delay in setting out the meal where nothing was required for display or effect, beyond the excellent quality of the food and its being well cooked. Maid-servants remained in attendance to brush off flies with *chauri* (fly-whiskers), to serve water and dishes. Before anyone touched the meal, water was carried round for each lady to wash the hands and rinse the mouth. It was deemed unclean to eat without this form of ablution. This done, the chief lady turned to her meal saying: '*Bismillah*' (In the name of God). They ate with the right hand and never used the left one. Although they partook of every variety of food placed before them with no other aid than their fingers, yet the mechanical habit was so perfect that they neither dropped a grain of rice, or soiled the dress, nor retained any of the food on their fingers. The lady was a little surprised and noted that everyone who witnessed (this feat) must admire the neat way in which eating was accomplished by these really 'children of nature'.

The dinner over, the *lota* (large, round vessel with water) and the *laggan* (large tray to receive the water after rinsing the hands and mouth) were passed round. Soap was not used (it was used only by washermen) and, instead, *besan* (fine flour of *chana-dal* = pulse of gram) was served for removing grease etc. from the fingers. Everyone rinsed her hands and mouth, and announced: '*Ash-Shukru'li-llah*' (All thanks to God) as soon as she finished.

Lota and *laggan* were of metal, either of brass, bronze or copper, tastefully lacquered over or, more frequently, in the household of nobility, of silver and gold with exquisite *minakari* (colour inlay). Every article of their daily used was an art-curio. China dishes, bowls and basins (*thalis*) were used for serving many of the savoury articles of food, though things of choice were served up in red earthen platters, as many delicacies, mostly milk preparations as *khir*, were esteemed more palatable from the earthen flavour (called *saundh*) of the new earthen vessel in which it was served.

The English lady imagined that the ladies of the *zenanah* were sadly deficient in actual comforts when she found, upon her first arrival in India (in the beginning of the 19th century A.D.), that there was no preparations for breakfast going forward and everyone seemed engaged in *pan*-eating and *huqah*-smoking. There was no breakfast after the morning namaz. She was, however, soon satisfied that they felt no sort of privation, as the early meal, so common in Europe, had never been introduced in India. Their first meal was a good substantial lunch at 10, 11 or 12 o'clock, after which followed *pan* and *huqqah*. An afternoon nap of two or three hours followed without impeding the prayers. The second meal (dinner) followed in twelve hours from the first and consisted of the same substantial fare. Finally they retired to sleep for the night.

(c) Mughal Cuisine

The dishes prepared in the *harem* could be classed under three heads:

(A) dishes in which no meat was used, i.e. *sufiyana* or pure vegetarian;

(B) dishes in which meat and rice were used; and

(C) dishes of meats cooked with spices, i.e. completely non-vegetarian.

Ingredients of ten recipies of each kind may be described.

(A) (1) *Zard Birinj*: rice, sugarcandy (*mishri*), *ghee* (clarified butter), raisins (*kishmish*), almond (*badam*) and pistachio *(pishta)*, salt, fresh ginger (*adrakh*), saffron (*keshar, zafran*) and cinnamon (*dalchini*).

(2) *Khushka*: rice and salt.

(3) *Khichri*: rice, *mung-dal* (mung-pulse), *ghee* and salt.

(4) *Shirbirinj*: milk, rice, sugarcandy and salt.

(5) *Thuli*: *maida* (fine wheat-flour), *ghee*, pepper (*kali-mirch*), cinnamon (*dalchini*), clove (*laung*), cardamom (*ilaychi*), salt, milk and *batashe* (bubbles of sugar).

(6) *Chikhi*: *maida* (fine wheat flour), spices, meat, *ghee*, onion (pyaz), saffron, cardamom, clove, cinnamon, round-pepper, coriander-seed (*dhaniya*), fresh ginger and salt.

(7) *Badinjan*: *maida*, *ghee*, onion, ginger, lime-juice, pepper, coriander-seed (*dhaniya*), clove, (cardamom) and asafoetida (*hing*).

(8) *Pahit*: *mung-dal, ghee*, salt, fresh ginger, cuminseed (*zira*) and asafoetida (*hing*); it was mostly eaten with *khushka*.

(9) *Sag*: spinach (*palak*), fennel (*soya*), *ghee*, onion, fresh ginger, pepper, cardamom and clove.

(10) *Halwa*: *suji* (coarse wheat flour), *ghee* and sugarcandy (*mishri*).

(B) (1) *Qabuli*: rice, meat, *ghee*, skinned gram, onion, salt, fresh ginger, cinnamon (*dalchini*), round pepper (*kali-mirch*), cuminseed (*zira*), cardamom (*ilaychi*), clove (*laung*), almond (*badam*) and raisins (*kishmish*).

(2) *Duzdbiryan*: rice, meat, *ghee*, and salt.

(3) *Qima Pulao*: rice, minced meat, *ghee*, peeled gram (*chana-dal*), onion, salt, fresh ginger, pepper, cuminseed (*zira*), cardamom (*ilaychi*) and clove (*laung*).

(4) *Shulla*: rice, meat, *ghee*, gram, salt, fresh ginger (*adarakh*), garlic (*lahsun*), round pepper, cinnamon (*dalchini*), cardamom (*ilaychi*) and clove (*laung*).

(5) *Bughra*: meat, wheat-flour, *ghee*, gram, vinegar (*sirka*), sugarcandy (*mishri*), onion (*pyaz*), carrot (*gajar*), beet (*chukandar*), turnip (*shaljam*), spinach (*palak*), fennel (*soya*), ginger (*adarakh*), saffron (*keshar*), clove (*laung*) cardamom (*ilaychi*), cuminseed (*zira*), cinnamon (*dalchini*) and round pepper (*kali mirch*).

(6) *Qima Shurba*: rice, meat, *ghee*, gram and all other ingredients of *Bughra*.

(7) *Harisa*: meat, *mash* (*daliya*, crushed wheat), *ghee*, salt and cinnamon (*dalchini*).

(8) *Kashk*: meat, crushed wheat (*daliya*), *ghee*, gram, salt, onion, ginger, cinnamon, saffron, clove, cardamom and cuminseed.

(9) *Halim*: meat, crushed wheat, *ghee*, gram, spices and saffron as in *Kashk*, and turnip (*shalgam*), carrot (*gajar*), spinach (*palak*) and fennel (*soya*).

(10) *Qutab* (*Sanbusa* or *Samosa*): meat, *maida* (fine

wheat flour), *ghee*, onion, fresh ginger, salt, pepper, coriander-seed (*dhaniya*), cardamom (*ilaychi*), cuminseed (*zira*), clove (*laung*) and *summaq*; this was cooked in twenty different ways.

(C) (1) *Biryan*: a full *Dashmandi* sheep, salt, *ghee*, saffron, clove, pepper and cuminseed (*zira*) which was cooked in different ways.

(2) *Yakhni* (broth): meat, onion and salt.

(3) *Yulma*: a full sheep was scalded in water till all the wool came off; it was then prepared like *yakhni*. A lamb was preferred owing to softness of flesh.

(4) *Kabab*: meat, *ghee*, salt, fresh ginger (*adarakh*), onion (*pyaz*), cuminseed (*zira*), coriander-seed (*dhaniya*), pepper (*kali mirch*), cardamom (*ilaychi*) and clove (*laung*). It was of various kinds.

(5) *Musamman*: all the bones of a fowl were taken out through the neck, the fowl remaining whole: minced meat, *ghee*, egg, onion, coriander (*dhaniya*), fresh ginger (*adarakh*), salt, round pepper (*kali mirch*) and saffron (*keshar*).

(6) *Dupiyaza*: meat that was medium fat, *ghee*, onion, salt, fresh pepper, cuminseed (*zira*), coriander-seed (*dhania*), cardamom (*ilaychi*), clove (*laung*) and pepper (*kali mirch*).

(7) *Mutanjana* sheep: meat that was medium fat, *ghee*, gram, ginger, cuminseed (*zira*), round pepper (*kali mirch*), clove (*laung*), cardamom (*ilaychi*), coriander-seed (*dhania*). It was also made from fowl and fish meat.

(8) *Dampukht*: meat, *ghee*, onion, fresh ginger (*adarakh*), pepper (*kali mirch*), clove (*laung*) and cardamom (*ilaychi*).

(9) *Qaliya*: minced meat (*qima*), *ghee*, onion, pepper, clove, cardamom and salt.

(10) *Malghuba*: meat, curd, *ghee*, onion, ginger and clove (*laung*).

Several kinds of bread (*roti*) were prepared in the kitchen. There was one bread of a large kind baked in an oven, made of flour, milk, *ghee* and salt. Smaller ones were also made. The thin kind was baked on an iron plate (*tawa*); fifteen were prepared from one *ser* of flour. There were various ways of making it. One kind was called *chapati*, which was sometimes made of *khushka*. It tasted very well when served hot. Finest flour reduced to fifty percent of wheat was used in the imperial kitchen. Only the best quality was obtained and 'purity' was the watchword. 'Adulteration' was not heard of during the Mughal times.

A large number of ready-made pickles (*achar*), the most favoured being those of lime (*nibu*), mango (*am*), carrot (*gajar*), onion (*pyaz*), garlic (*lahsun*), chilli (*mirch*), radish (*muli*), ginger (*adrakh*), *labhera* (*lisaura*) and *aonla* (*amla*), and *murabbas* (deshi jams) of choicest fruits were used by the ladies of the *harem*. These too were under the charge of the kitchen establishment.

Nothing like 'fast foods' were used in the Mughal *harem*. Dry fruits, ready-made sweets and fried *namkins* (spiced grain preparation) were abundantly available in the palace for casual snacks. Such sweets as *balu-shahi*, *jalebi*, *imarti* and *khurma*, and the famous *dal-moth* of Agra were the inventions of the medieval period. Fresh fruits as musk-melon (*kharbuza*), apple (*seb*), grape (*angur*), fig (*anjir*), date (*khajur*), pear (*naspati*), peach (*shaftalu*) and apricot (*khubani*) were despatched from regions as distant as Kashmir, Chaman, Qandahar, Kabul, Bukhara and Samarqand by the *ḍak-chowki* system or by trading *banjaras*, for regular supply in the *harem*. The ladies and in no less degree the king and his nobles, were however mostly fond of the seasonal fruits like mango (*am*), musk-melon and water melon (*kharbuza* and *tarbuz*), orange (*santara*), *singhara*, *kaseru*, pomegranate (*anar*), banana (*kela*), citron (*chakotara*), blackberry (*jamun*), custard-apple, mulberry (*shahtut*), guava (*amrud*), *khirni* and *phalsa* which were locally obtained in large quantities and regularly supplied in the *harem*. The seasonal fruits were invariably patronised by the *harem* inmates, almost as a rule, on health grounds as prescribed by the *hakims* (physicians) of the age for proper synchronisation of human biology with nature.

The following is a list of fruits and their prices in Akbar's age (c. 1600 A.D.).

Turani (imported) Fruits & Dry Fruits

Arhang Kharbuza (*Sarda*)		
(Melon) 1st Quality	-	2½ *rupiya* per melon
Arhang Kharbuza (2nd quality)	-	1 to 2½
Kabul *Kharbuza* (1st quality)	-	1 to 1½
Kabul *Kharbuza* (2nd quality)	-	¾ to 1
Kabul *Kharbuza* (3rd quality)	-	½ to ¾
Samarqand apples	-	1 *rupiya* for 7 to 15
Sharifa (*Shriphal*) (quinces)	-	1 *rupiya* for 10 to 30

Anar (pomegranates)	-	6 ½ to 15 *rupiya* per *man*
Amrud (guava)	-	1 *rupiya* for 10 to 100
Kabul and European apples	-	1 *rupiya* for 5 to 10
Kashmir grapes	-	108 *dam* per *man*
Khajur (date)	-	10 *dam* per *ser*
Kishmish (raisins)	-	9 *dam* per *ser*
Abjosh (large raisins)	-	9 *dam* per *ser*
Ber (plum)	-	8 *dam* per *ser*
Khubani (dried apricot)	-	8
Qandahar dry grapes	-	7
Anjir (fig)	-	7
Munaqqa (large raisins)	-	6¾
Unnao (jujube)	-	3½
Badam (almond) without shell	-	28
Badam (almond) with shell	-	11
Pishta (pistachio) without shell	-	16
Pishta (pistachio) with shell	-	9
Chilghuza nuts	-	8
Sinjid (jujube)	-	6½
Jawz (nut) without shell	-	4½
Girdgan (walnut)	-	2½

Sweet Fruits of Hindustan

Am (mango)	-	10 to 40 *dam* per 100
Anannas (pine apple)	-	4 *dam* for 1
Kawta (an orange)	-	1 *dam* for 2

Ganna (sugarcane)	-	1 *dam* for 2
Kathal (jackfruit)	-	1 *dam* for 2
Kela (banana)	-	1 *dam* for 2
Ber (plum)	-	2 *dam* per *ser*
Anar (pomegranate)	-	80 to 100 *dam* per *man*
Amrud (guava)	-	1 *dam* for 2
Anjir (fig)	-	1 *dam* per *ser*
Shahtut (mulberry)	-	2 *dam* per *ser*
Sharifa (Sitaphal) (custard apple)	-	1 *dam* for 1
Kharbuza (melon)	-	40 *dam* per *man*
Tarbuz (water melon)	-	2 to 10 *dam* for 1
Khirni	-	4 *dam* per *ser*
Mahuwa	-	1 *dam* per *ser*
Dephal	-	4
Tendu	-	2 *dam* per *ser*
Khajur (date)	-	4
Malshri (*Bholsari*)	--	4
Tarkul	-	1 *dam* for 2
Paniyala	-	2 *dam* per *ser*
Lahsaura (*Labhera*)	-	1
Gumbhi	-	4
Karahri	-	4
Banga	-	1 *dam* for 2
Gular	-	2 *dam* per *ser*
Pilu	-	2
Piyar	-	4

Hindustani Dry Fruits

Nariyal (coconut)	-	4 *dam* for 1
Chhuhara (dry dates)	-	6 *dam* per *ser*
Akharot (walnut)	-	8
Chiraunji	-	4
Makhana	-	4
Supari (betelnut)	-	8
Kamalgatta	-	2

Vegetables

Parwal (*Palwal*)	-	2 *dam* per *ser*
Kaddu or Kasiphal (pumpkin)	-	2½ *dam* for 1
Badinjan	-	1½ *dam* per *ser*
Turai	-	1½
Kanduri	-	1½
Sem	-	1½
Petha	-	1½
Karela	-	1½
Kakora	-	1½
Kachalu	-	2
Chachinda	-	2
Suran	-	1 *dam* per *ser*
Gajar (carrot)	-	1
Singhara	-	3
Salak	-	2

Pindalu	-	2 *dam* per *ser*
Keseru	-	3

Sour & Acidic Fruits

Nibu (lime)	-	1 *dam* for 4
Amalbet	-	1 *dam* for 4
Galgal	-	1 *dam* for 2
Bijaura	-	8 *dam* for 1
Amla (*Awla* or *Anwla*)	-	2 *dam* per *ser*
Imli (*Ambili*) (tamarind)	-	2 *dam* per *ser*
Badhal	-	1 *dam* for 1
Kamrakh	-	1 *dam* for 4
Narangi (orange)	-	1 *dam* for 2
Jamun (blackberry)	-	1 *dam* per *ser*
Phalsa	-	1½ *dam* per *ser*
Karaunda	-	1 *dam* per *ser*
Kait	-	1 *dam* for 4
Pakar	-	½ *dam* per *ser*
Karna	-	1 *dam* for 1
Janbhiri	-	1 *dam* for 5

Mangoes and melons were most relished. A wide variety of mangoes was available. *Faludas* or mixtures of the slices of these fruits and scented syrups (*sherbets* = sweet cold drinks) were also very popular in summer. *Khas*, *kewda* and *gulab* were the most favoured flavours.

An idea of the vastness of this establishment can be made by the fact that a separate department of drinking water and ice was maintained. It was called the *Abdar-Khanah.* Akbar attached great importance to this department and committed it to the care of trusted and competent persons. Whether at home or on travel, he always drank Ganga water (*Gangajal*) only. Adequate arrangement was made for its regular supply. Some trustworthy persons were stationed on the banks of the river Ganga. They despatched the water in sealed jars daily. When the court was at Agra and Fatehpur Sikri (1560-85), the water came from Soron, near Kasganj-Etah (Uttar Pradesh), and it travelled by carts. When Akbar was residing in Lahore (Punjab) (1585-96), Ganga water was brought from Hardwar. Obviously he attached greater importance to the water of Ganga than that of Yamuna or Ravi, and this he did, not out of some superstitious belief, but owing to the excellent quality of the Ganga water from the health point of view. For cooking food, rain water or water taken from the Yamuna and the Chenab was mixed with a little Ganga water. On journeys and hunting parties Akbar, from his predilection for good water, appointed experienced men as water-tasters.

Jehangir travelled to distant regions like Kabul, Kashmir, Ajmer, Ahmedabad and Mandu and he mostly lived in the camp. He could not stick to the use of Ganga water, which he always admired the most. But wherever he went, he preferred natural flowing water of a river or rivulet to a settled well, *baoli* or tank water. Once he had the waters of a particular region carefully weighed to ascertain the lightest of them. So particular were the Mughals about their drinking water, which is in fact the real source of life.

Shah Jehan has also been recorded to drink only Yamuna-water which was pure, clean and perfectly potable in the medieval period. Though sweet well water was available both in the Agra Fort and the Red Fort, Delhi, he always drank Yamuna water. When Aurangzeb besieged him in Agra Fort and cut off its water supply from the river, in 1658, he could not drink any other water available in the fort, so accustomed to the 'molten snow' of the Yamuna he was, and urged by his thirst in the burning heat of June, he wrote the following touching letter to his cruel son:

> My son, my hero!
> Why should I complain of the unkindness of Fortune,
> Seeing that not a leaf is shed by a tree, without God's Will?
> Only yesterday I was master of nine hundred thousand
> Troopers and today I am in need of a pitcher of water!
> Praised be the Hindus in all cases,
> As they even offer water to their dead,
> And thou, my son, art a marvellous Musalman,
> As thou causest me in life to lament for water!

To this appeal of his old and sick father, Aurangzeb, the 'marvellous Musalman', sent the brutal reply: 'It is your own doing.' For three days Shah Jehan held out. Then, 'amidst raging thirst with only despair and treason around him he decided to surrender' and opened the gates of Agra Fort to Aurangzeb on June 8 1658. He was confined within the *harem* quarters where he died after eight years in 1666.

It must be noted that though, by and large, Agra has brackish water, there are a large number of wells and *baolis*, some of them being in the fort itself, which had, until recently, extremely sweet, healthy and potable water. The famous Kuan Kamal Khan, where Jehangir installed as many as 32 *purs* and where he stayed with his vast camp, was a great reservoir of sweet water relished by him.

Copper or earthen pots called *kalash* and *ghada* were used to store water. Saltpetre (*shora*) was used as a means for cooling water. It is saline earth. A perforated vessel was filled with it. Some water was poured over it and whatever dropped through was collected. It was then boiled, cleaned and left to crystallise. Pure saltpetre was thus obtained. One *ser* of water was then put into a goglet of pewter, or silver, or any other such metal, and the mouth closed. Then two and half *sers* of saltpetre was thrown into a vessel, together with five *sers* of water, and in this mixture the goglet was stirred about for a quarter of an hour when the water in the goglet cooled.

Snow and ice came into use since 1586 when Akbar went to the Punjab. Ice was brought by land and water, by post carriages or bearers, from the district of Panhan, in the northern mountains, about 45 *kos* (= 90 miles = 144 kms) from Lahore. The dealers derived a considerable profit, two or three *sers* of ice being sold per rupee (*rupiya*), in an age when ten rupees could purchase one *tola* of gold; when pistachio without shell was sold at six *dam* per *ser* = 6½ *sers* per rupee (40 *dam* = one rupee) so that ice was the costliest luxury. The greatest profit was derived when ice was brought by water, next when by carriages, and least when by bearers. The inhabitants of the mountains brought it in loads, and sold in piles of 25 to 30 *sers* at the rate of five *dams* per *ser*. If they had to bring it very far, the price was 24 *dam* 17 *jital;* if the distance was average the price was 15 *dam*.

Out of the ten boats employed for the transport of ice, one arrived daily at the capital, each being maned by four boatmen. The bundles contained six to twelve *sers* of ice, according to the temperature. A carriage brought two loads. There were fourteen stages, where the horses were changed and, besides, one elephant was used. Twelve bundles of four to ten *sers* arrived daily. By this kind of transport, a *ser* of ice costed in winter 3 *dam* 21 *jital;* during the rains 14 *dam* 20 *jital;* in the intermediate time 9 *dam* 21½ *jital;* and in the average 5 *dam* 15½ *jital.* If it was brought by bearers, 28 men were required for the 14 stages. They brought one load every day, containing four parcels. In the beginning of the year, the ice costed 5 *dam* 19½ *jital;* in the middle 16 *dam* 2 1/8 *jital;* and in the end 19 *dam* 15 5/8 *jital* per *ser;* in the average the rate was at 8 7/8 *dam* per *ser.* All ranks attached to the *darbar* used ice in summer which was regularly supplied by the traders. The nobles (*mansabdars*) used it as a costly luxury throughout the year.

---

* **Table of Currency (used in Akbar's time)**

8	*damri* (copper coin)	= 1 *dam*
25	*jital* (it was just a theoretical denomination for accounting to 1000th part of a *rupiya*)	= 1 *dam*
40	*dam*	= 1 *rupiya* (silver rupee)
10	*rupiya*	= 1 gold *muhr* (of one *tola* = 11.66 gms)

* **Table of Weights (used in Akbar's age)**

1	*tola*	= 180 grains or 11.66 grams (1 gram = 15.44 grains)
1	*dam* (also used as a weight)	= 324 grains or 1.8 *tol*
30	*dam*	= 1 *ser* (= 9720 grains or 630 grams or 54 *tolas*)

		Thus 1 Akbari *ser* was of 54 *tolas* and not of the later 80 *tolas*.
40 *ser*	=	1 *man* (= 2160 *tolas* or 25.2 kilograms)

7

Mughal Perfumes & Incenses

Akbar and his successors were very fond of perfumes both for using on the person and for burning in the household and the court-hall which were continually scented with *ambar* (ambergris), *agar* (aloewood) and other incenses. Some of these were definitely ancient recipes which the Hindus had been popularly using in their temples, while some compositions were invented by Akbar himself, as his historian has recorded. Incenses were daily burnt in the *harem* in gold and silver censers of various beautiful shapes and designs. Besides these, sweet-smelling flowers were used in large quantities. *Araqs*, *itrs* and oils were also extracted from flowers and used for skin and hair.

Akbar created a separate department called *Khushbu-Khanah* (Department of Perfumery). Shah Mansur was put in charge of it.

Some of the choicest recipes were as follows:

(1) *Santuk* was used for keeping the skin fresh. It was prepared from *zabad* (civet), *chuwa, chambeli* essence and rose-water.

(2) *Argaja* was used in summer for keeping the skin cool. It was prepared from *chandan* (sandalwood), *iksir, mid chuwa, banafsha* (violet-root), *gehla, kapur* (camphor) and *'arq of rose* (rose-water; *gulab-jal*).

(3) *Gulkama* was an incense prepared by a special process from *ambar* (ambergris), *ladan, mushk* (*kasturi*), *agar* (aloewood), *iksir-i-'abir,* juice of *Gul-i-surkh,* rose-water, extract of *bahar* and juice of *bahar-i-naranj.*

(4) *Ruh-Afza* was also burnt in censers and gave a very fine smell (*khushbu, sugandha*) in the household. It was prepared from *agar* (aloewood), *chandan* (sandalwood), *ladan, iksir, loban, dhup, banafsha* (violet-root), *chharila* and rose-water.

(5) *Opatna* was a scented soap, made by an intricate process of *ladan, agar* (aloewood), *bahar-i-naranj* and its bark, *chandan* (sandalwood), *chhar, chharila, mushk, pacha* leaves, apples, *moth,* violet-root, *dhup, ikanki, kachur, loban,* rose-water and extract of *bahar.*

(6) *Abirmaya* was prepared from *agar* (aloewood), *chandan* (sandalwood), violet-root, *chhar, dawalak, mushk, ladan, bahar-i-naranj* and rose-water. It was used as a soap.

(7) *Kishta* smelt very fine when burnt and was exhilarating. It was prepared from *agar* (aloewood), *ladan, lobal, chandan* (sandalwood),

iksir, dhup, violet-root, *mushk, chharila* and rose-water.

(8) *Bukhur* was also an incense made of *agar* (aloewood), *chandan* (sandalwood), *ladan, mushk, iksir,* refined sugar and rose-water.

(9) *Fatila* was an incense prepared from *agar* (aloewood), *chandan* (sandalwood), *iksir, ladan,* violet-root, *loban,* refined sugar and rose-water.

(10) *Barjat* was a soap made of *agar* (aloewood), *ladan, mushk, chandan* (sandalwood), *loban* and *kapur* (camphor).

(11) *Abir-Iksir* was a soap prepared from *chandan* (sandalwood), *iksir and mushk.*

(12) *Ghasul* was liquid soap made of *chandan* (sandalwood), *katul, mushk, chuwa, kapur* (camphor), *mid* and rose-water.

The ingredients of these perfume-recipes were obtained from various sources from distant regions. *Ambar* (ambergris) was a marine-product. *Ladan* was extracted from a tree which grew in Cyprus and the Mediterranean regions. *Kapur* (camphor) was also a tree-extract. *Zabad,* also called *shakh* (civet) was an animal product obtained from Achin. *Gaura* was also an animal product brought from Achin. *Mid* was prepared from an animal secretion. *Agar,* wood of aloe, also called Ud, was the root of a tree. It came from Gujarat, Achin and Dhanasari. *Chuwa* was distilled from wood of *agar* by an intricate process. *Chandan* (sandalwood) came from China and South India. *Silaras* was the gum of a tree which was grown in Turkey. *Kalanbak* (calembic) was the wood of a tree which came from Zirbad. *Malagir* was also a tree-wood. *Loban* (frank-incense) was an odorous gum of a tree which was found in Java. *Azfar-ut-Tib* was the house of an animal which had a sweet smell as the animal fed on *sumbul.*

It was found in India, Basrah and Bahrayan. *Gugal* or *sugandh-gugala* was a very common plant of India. These were thus natural, and either of vegetation or animal products and were harmless, in contradiction to the modern synthetic and chemical scents and soaps. *Agar, chandan* and *kapur,* the three most frequently used ingredients were indigenous and these were tree products. Others were imported, practically from all over the medieval orient. That the medieval people spent so enormously on their luxuries is not surprising, as they could very well afford it.

The following fine smelling (*khushbudar*) flowers were largely patronised:

1. *Sewti*
2. *Malshri* (*molshri* or *bholsari*)
3. *Chameli* or *Chambeli* (jasmine)
4. *Ray-Bel*
5. *Mongra* (also called *motia*)
6. *Champa* (magnolia)
7. *Ketki* (pandanus)
8. *Juhi*
9. *Nargis* (narcissus)
10. *Kewra*
11. *Singarhar* or *Harsinghar*
12. *Banafsha* (violet)
13. *Karna*
14. *Kapur-bel*
15. *Gul-i-Zafaran*
16. *Chalta*

17. *Gulab* (rose)
18. *Kamal* (lotus)
19. *Kamalini* (*Kumudini*) (lily)
20. *Tasbih-Gulal*
21. *Kuza*
22. *Padal*
23. *Niwari*
24. *Hinna*
25. *Malti* etc.

Some of the most fragrant of these were also used for making oils and scents. *'Araqs* or extracts were made during Akbar's time. *Gulab-jal* and *kewra-jal* (extracted from *gulab* and *kewra* respectively) were popularly used, e.g. in the presentation of various dishes of the kitchen.

Jehangir claimed that *'itr* (attar or otto) was a discovery of his reign. He ascribed it to Asmat Begum, mother of Nur Jehan and noted in his diary:

> I have regret for the *Jahangiri-'Itr* (or *Itr-i-Jahangiri*) that my father (Akbar's) nostrils were not gratified with such essences. This *'itr* is a discovery which was made during my reign through the efforts of the mother of Nur Jehan Begum. When she was making rose-water, a scum formed on the surface of the dishes into which the hot rose-water was poured from the jugs. She collected this scum little by little; when much rose-water was obtained a considerable portion of the scum was collected. It is of such strength in

> perfume that if one drop be rubbed on the palm of the hand, it scents a whole assembly and it appears as if many red rose-buds had bloomed at once. There is no other scent of equal excellence to it. It restores hearts that have gone, and brings back withered souls. In reward for that invention, I presented a string of pearls to the inventress.

Henceforth, the use of *'itrs* became very popular in the *harem* and the court. Different *'itrs* were used on the person according to the season. Gradually perfumes became a characteristic feature of the lifestyle of the Mughals and of those who emulated them and could afford this costly luxury. The later Mughals used *'itrs* so wantonly that they are credited to have flown them into *harem* cascades, tanks and fountains and virtually bathed with them.

The following is an authoritative list of perfumes and their prices in Akbar's reign (c. 1600 A.D.):

1.	*'Ambar-i-Ashhab*	- 1 to 3 gold *muhrs* per *tola*
2.	*Zabad* (Civet)	- ½ *rupiya* to 1 *gold muhr* per *tola*
3.	*Mushk*	- 1 to 4½ *rupiya* per *tola*
4.	*Agar*	- 2 *rupiya* to 1 *gold muhr* per *ser*
5.	*Chuwa*	- $^{1}/_{8}$ to 1 *rupiya* per *tola*
6.	*Gaura*	- 3 to 5 *rupiya* per *tola*
7.	*Bhimseni Kapur*	- 3 *rupiya* to 2 gold *muhr* per *ser*
8.	*Mid*	- 1 to 3 *rupiya* per *tola*
9.	*Zafaran*	- 12 to 22 *rupiya* per *ser*
10.	*Zafaran-i-Kamandi*	- 1 to 3 *muhrs* per *ser*
11.	*Zafaran-i-Kashmir*	- 8 to 12 *rupiya* per *ser*

12. *Chandan* - 32 to 55 *rupiya* per *man*
13. *Kalanbak* - 10 to 40 *rupiya* per *man*
14. *Silaras* - 3 to 5 *rupiya* per *ser*
15. *'Ambar-i-Ladan* - 1½ to 4 *rupiya* per *ser*
16. *Kafur-i-China* - 1 to 2 *rupiya* per *ser*
17. *'Araq-i-Fitna* - 1 to 3 *rupiya* per *bottle*
18. *'Araq-i-Bed-i-Mushk* - 1 to 4 *rupiya* per *bottle*
19. *'Araq-i-Gulab* - ½ to 1 *rupiya* per *bottle*
20. *'Araq-i-Bahar* - 1 to 5 *rupiya* per *bottle*
21. *'Araq-i-Chambeli* - 1/8 to ¼ *rupiya per bottle*
22. *Banafsha* - ½ to 1 *rupiya* per *ser*
23. *Azfar-ut-Tib* - 1½ to 2
24. *Barg-i-Maj* - ½ to 1
25. *Gugal* - 10 to 13
26. *Loban-i-Sargard* - 1/3 to 3 *rupiya* per *tola*
27. *Loban* - 1 to 2 *rupiya* per *ser*
28. *Chhar* - ¼ to ½
29. *Chharila* - 3 to 4 *dam* per *ser*

8
Mughal Addictions and Intoxicants

(a) Wine and Opium

Babur, the founder of the Mughal dynasty in India, was addicted to *araq* (wine) and *ma'jun* (a confection or concoction of opium), and he used one or both regularly. There are numerous references to his addictions in his *Memoirs*. Thus, he recorded the interesting event of a drinking party held at Bhira (Punjab) on March 5, 1519 as follows:

Next morning when the court rose, we rode out for an excursion, entered a boat and there drank *'araq*. The people of the party were Khwaja Dost-Khawand, Khusrau, Mirim, Mirza Quli, Muhammadi, Ahmadi, Gadai, Na'man, Langar Khan, Rauh-Dam, Qasim-i-'Ali (*Tariyaki* = the opium eater), Yusuf-i-'Ali and Tingri Quli. Towards the head of the boat there was a *talar* (platform or pavilion), on the flat roof of which I sat with a few people, a few others sitting below. There was a sitting place also at the tail of the boat; there Muhammadi, Gadai and Na'man sat. *'Araq* was drunk till the other prayer (time) when, disgusted by its (*'araq's*) bad flavour, by consent of those at the head of the boat, *ma'jun* was preferred. Those at the other end, knowing nothing about our *ma'jun*, drank *'araq* right through. At the bed-time prayer, we rode from the boat and got into camp late. Thinking I had been drinking *'araq*, Muhammadi and Gadai said to one another: 'Let us do a befitting service', and lifting a pitcher of *'araq* up to one another in turn on their horses, came in, speaking together with wonderful joviality and heartiness, 'Through this dark night have we come carrying this pitcher in turns'. Later on when they knew that the party was meant to be otherwise (and we had been taking *ma'jun*), they were much disturbed because never did a *ma'jun* party go well with a drinking party. I said, 'Don't upset the party. Let those who wish to drink *'araq*, drink *'araq;* let those who wish to eat *ma'jun*, eat *ma'jun*. Let no one on either side make talk or allusion to the other.' Some drank *'araq*, some ate *ma'jun* and for a time the party went on quite politely. Baba Jan, the *qabuz-player*, had not been there in our party in the boat. We invited him now when he reached the tents. He asked to drink *'araq*. We invited Tardi Muhammad *Qibchaq* also and made him a comrade of the drinkers. A *ma'jun* party never

> goes well with an *'araq* or wine party; the drinkers began to make wild talk and chatter from all sides, mostly in allusion to *ma'jun* and *ma'junis* (addicts of *ma'jun*). Baba Jan even, when drunk, said many wild things. The drinkers soon made Tardi Khan mad-drunk, by giving him one full bowl after another. Try as we did to keep things straight, nothing went well. There was much disgusting uproar. The party became intolerable and was broken up.

This fully illustrates his addiction both to wine and opium, which he greatly enjoyed in the company of his friends, colleagues and senior nobles.

He has recorded another episode of a wine-party, held on November 14, 1519 at Kabul:

> I rode out of the *char-bagh* at midnight, sent night-watch and groom back, crossed Mulla Baba's bridge, got out by the Diurin-narrows, round by the *bazars* and *karez* of Qush-Nadur, along the back of the Bear-house, and near sun-rise reached Tardi Berg *Khaksar's karez.* He ran out quickly on hearing of me. I gave him 100 *shahrukhis* and told him to get wine and other things ready as I had a fancy for a private and unrestrained (wine) party. ... At the first watch (9.00 a.m.) Tardi Beg brought a pitcher of wine which we drank by turns. After him, came Muhammad-i-Qasim Barlas and Shah-Zada who had got to know of his fetching the wine, and had followed him. We invited them to the party. Said Tardi Beg, 'Hul-Hul Aniga wishes to drink wine with you.' I said, 'For my part, I never saw a woman drink wine; invite her'. We also invited Shahi, a *qalandar,* and one of the

karez-men who played the rebeck. There was drinking till the evening prayer on the rising ground behind the *karez;* we then went into Tardi Beg's house and drank by lamp-light almost till the bed-time prayer. The party was quite free and unpretending (informal). I lay down; the others went to another house and drank there till the beat of the drum (midnight). Hul-Hul Aniga came in and made much disturbance. I got rid of her at last by flinging myself down as if drunk. It was in my mind to put people off their guard and ride off alone to Astar-Ghach, but it did not come off because they got to know. In the end, I rode away at the beat of the drum, after letting Tardi Beg and Shah-Zada know.

Babur was a poet and he is recorded to have composed the following lines on his addiction to wine:

Nauroz va naubahar va ma'y,
Va dilbari khusht,
Babur ba'aish kush ki,
'Alam dubarah na'-ast.

(The New Year, the spring, the wine and the beloved are pleasing, O Babur enjoy them, for the world is not to be had a second time).

These references by his own pen show that addiction to wine and opium was a regular feature of his life. Saturday, Sunday, Tuesday and Wednesday were marked as 'drinking days' when they (Babur and his associates) drank wine, while on non-drinking days (i.e. Monday, Thursday and Friday) there were parties for *ma'jun.* He used them regularly, probably as stimulant rather than for intoxication, owing to his extremely hard and difficult life in the field and constant exertion on his body and strain on his mind. Without it perhaps he could not sleep. The addiction was prevalent among the nobility, and even ladies indulged in it.

It may be recalled that on the eve of the battle of Khanwa in 1527, when the Mughals were facing a much larger and mightier army of Rana Sanga, Babur proclaimed to renounce wine which was flown on the ground and their vessels were broken. This determination had a statutory effect on his army, which he ultimately led to victory.

Humayun was addicted to opium and he took wine only rarely, just for company's sake. He was excessively fond of opium and could not do without this intoxicant. He used to say that he was an opium-eater (*afion-chi* or *afimchi*) and if there was any delay in his timings, people should not mind it. This had, in fact, made him ease-loving, lazy and lethargic and he lost many a good initiative, both political and military, owing to this addiction. In comparison, his son Akbar was disciplined and restrained. He drank a little, within reasonable measures so that he was always 'sober in his cups'. He was also accustomed to taking opium in the form of drink. It was called *post,* a preparation of opium, diluted and modified by various admixtures of spices. He used to take it as a tonic for health and as a stimulant, rather than for intoxication. It was about the same time that various concoctions of opium, e.g. *filuniya* and *'amal* were secretly introduced into the *harem* and the ladies, most prone to it in the circumstances in which they were set, took to this addiction on a large scale as a succour. Wine was introduced into the *harem* much later, in the early 18th century A.D.

In his addiction to wine and opium, Jehangir surpassed his ancestors. He began drinking when he was hardly seventeen and gradually became addicted to wine, opium and other drugs, some of which certainly had aphrodisiac effects. He has himself given an account of his addictions in his diary (*Memoirs*) of the year 1615-16. He noted that he drank for the first time on the bank of the river Indus after an arduous hunt when he was very tired. He found it very agreeable. After that he took to drinking wine and increased it from day to day until wine made from grapes ceased to intoxicate him and he took to drinking *arrack* (*'araq*, spirits) and by degrees, during nine years, his potions rose to twenty cups of doubly distilled spirits: fourteen during the day-time and six at night. The weight of this was 6 Hindustani ser or 1½ *maunds* of Iran. The quantity of his eating in those days was a fowl with bread and vegetables. In that state, no one had the courage to forbid him (from this course) and matters went to such a length that in the crapulous state from the excessive trembling of hand, he could not drink from his own cup and others had to give it to him to drink, until the wise physician Hakim Humam was consulted. He advised sincerely, that by the way he drank, the matters will come to such a pass in six months that there will be no remedy for it. This honest warning impressed him and from that day he began to lessen the quantity of wine and take *filuniya* (a drug or concoction of opium). In proportion, he went on diminishing liquor and increasing the amount of *filuniya*. He also ordered that the *arrack* should be diluted with wine of grape so that there should be two parts wine and one part *arrack*. Thus, in the course of seven years he brought it down to six cups. The weight of each cupful was 18¼ *misqals*. For fifteen years, he drank at this fixed rate. He drank at night, except on Thursday, as it was the day of the blessed accession. He did not drink also on Friday, the most blessed day of the week. He drank at the end of each day with these two exceptions. He did not eat meat on Thursday and Sunday, the former being the day of his accession and the latter being the birthday of his revered father. After some time, he substituted opium for *filuniya*. When he was about forty-seven, he ate eight *surkhs* (*rattis*, a red berry used as a weight) of opium when five *gharis* of the day had passed and six *surkhs* after one watch of the night.

Excessive use of intoxicants was constantly affecting his health and he had to finally regulate the quantity of the liquor to a minimum. He recorded in 1618 that he drank six cups of wine daily each of 7½ *tolas* (= 45 *tolas* = 524.7 grams). He further reduced it to six cups of 6 *tolas* and 3 *mashas* (= 37½ *tolas* = 437.25 grams) per day. This too was excessive by any standard and it ultimately ruined his health and numbered his days. Mostly he used to drink in the company of his trusted nobles and personal friends in the *Ghusl-Khanah* (*Shah-Burj*), but at times he also drank in the *harem* along with his ladies.

Several types of liquor were brewed for the commoners, e.g. *tari* from juice of coconut, palm or date trees; *nira* from araquier tree; *mahua; kherra; bhadwar; jagree* and *toddy.* Good wines for the royalty and nobility were imported from Persia and Portugal. Persian wine was brewed from grape. *'Araq* was also a superior wine manufactured from grape.

Shah Jehan was also fond of wine but he always drank with control and restraint, and in private. He is recorded to have given up wine during the Deccan campaign. The entire stock of wine was thrown into the Chambal and precious cups of gold and silver were broken and distributed among the poor and the needy. Aurangzeb totally abstained from it and he 'drank nothing except water.' In 1668 he issued strict orders prohibiting the use of intoxicating liquors, though this edict was hardly effective. The Mughal nobility could not do without it and they indulged in this addiction privately. Though the use of opium had considerably decreased, wine was a popular intoxicant of the rich and they could even afford to get it from the foreign travellers, as the latter have frequently recorded. The later Mughals crossed all limits of decency and not only did they drink wine with mugs and bowls from ponds filled with it, they also rejoiced in flowing it in the fountains of their apartments and virtually bathing in it. This is how opulence without intellectual discipline becomes debased.

(b) Tobacco and Huqah

Tobacco was introduced in northern India towards the close of Akbar's reign (c. 1604-5 A.D.). Asad Beg, Akbar's emissary to the court of Ibrahim 'Adil Shah-II of Bijapur, is reported to have brought it from the Deccan where it was introduced by the Portuguese. He recorded in his memoirs that he found tobacco in Bijapur. Never having seen the like in India, he brought some with him and prepared a handsome pipe of jewel-work. The stem, the finest to be procured at Achin, was three cubits in length, beautifully dried and coloured, both ends being adorned with jewels and enamel. He happened to come across a very handsome mouth-piece of Yaman cornelian, oval-shaped, which was set to the stem, the whole was very handsome. This was the earliest form of *huqah* (hubble bubble). There was also a golden burner (*chilam*) for lighting it as a proper accompaniment. 'Adil Khan had given him a betelbag of very superior workmanship; this he filled with fine tobacco, such, that if one leaf be lit, the whole will continue burning. All this apparatus he arranged elegantly on a silver tray. He had a silver tube made to keep the stem in, and that too was covered with purple velvet. This was presented along with other articles to Akbar.

When the king saw it he was surprised. He examined the tobacco which was made up in pipefuls and made inquiries about it. Nawab Khan-i-'Azam replied that it was tobacco which was well known in Mecca and Medina and it was a medicine for His Majesty. Akbar looked at it and ordered Asad Beg to prepare and give him a pipeful. He began to smoke it, when his physician approached and forbade him to smoke it. But the king was graciously pleased to say that he must smoke a little to gratify Asad Beg, and taking the mouthpiece into his mouth, drew two or three breaths. The physician was in great trouble, and would not let him do more. He took the pipe from his mouth and bid the Khan-i-'Azam to try it, who took two or three puffs. He then sent for his druggist, and asked what were its peculiar qualities. He replied that there was no mention of it in his books. It was a new invention, and the stems were imported from China. The European doctors had written much in its praise. The physician said that this was an untried medicine, about which their doctors had written nothing. How could they describe to His Majesty the qualities of such unknown things? It was not fitting that His Majesty should try it. Asad Beg replied to him that the Europeans were not so foolish as not to know all about it. There were wise men among them who seldom err or commit mistakes. How could you, before you had tried a thing and found out all its qualities, pass a judgement on it that could be depended on by the physicians, kings, great men and nobles? Things must be judged according to their good or bad qualities, and the decision must be according to the facts of the case. But the physician did not agree and replied that they did not want to follow the Europeans and adopt a custom which is not sanctioned by their wise men, without trial. Asad Beg did not relent and pleaded that every custom in the world had been new at one time or the other and from the days of Adam till now, they had been gradually invented. When a new thing was introduced among a people and became well known in the world, everyone adopted it. Wise men and physicians should determine according to the good or bad qualities of a thing. The good qualities may not appear at once. Thus the China-root not known anciently had been newly discovered and was useful in many diseases. The emperor was much pleased by this reasoning and blessed him. He said to Khan-i-'Azam that they must not reject a thing that had been adopted by the wise men of other nations merely because they could not find it in their books.

Otherwise, how should we progress? The king thus approved the use of tobacco and *huqah*.

Asad Beg noted that he had brought a large supply of tobacco and pipes. He sent some to several of the nobles, while others sent to ask for some. Indeed, all, without exception, wanted some, and the practice was introduced to the Mughals. After that, the merchants began to sell it, so that the custom of smoking *huqah* spread rapidly. Akbar used it very sparingly. Presumably, it was also introduced into the *harem*, about the same time, preferably for the use of the elderly ladies.

Huqah-smoking became very popular among the nobles. Jehangir disapproved the practice owing to its bad smell and indecent effects and he is recorded to have prohibited *huqah* and tobacco in 1617. He noted in his *Memoirs* that in consequence of the disturbance that tobacco brought about in most temperaments and constitutions, he ordered that no one should smoke it. Shah Abbas of Iran was also aware of the mischief arising from it and he had also prohibited it in Iran. But only in a decade's time, the Mughal nobles had become addicted to it and the decree was more honoured in its breach than observance. Jehangir has himself recorded an episode related to this addiction. Khan-i-'Alam, his ambassador to Persia was an addict of *huqah*-smoking which he practised continuously. When it was represented to Shah Abbas that Khan-i-'Alam could never be a moment without tobacco, Shah Abbas wrote a couplet of warning to him:

The friend's envoy wished to exhibit tobacco,
With fidelity's lamp, I light up the tobacco market.

To this Khan-i-'Alam replied,

I, poor wretch, was miserable at the tobacco notice,

By the just Shah's favour the tobacco-market became brisk.

The addiction of *huqah*-smoking gradually spread far and wide and the commoners also adopted it in a large measure. It became a popular pastime as much as an addiction.

Late 18th and early 19th century records show that *huqah* was in general use in the *zenanah* (ladies' apartments) of the nobles and the rich. An attendant called *huqah-bardar* (the bearer of *huqah*) was employed to keep it constantly going on. It was a common practice with the lady of the house to present the *huqah* to her favoured guest as a mark of honour. Youngsters did not smoke huqah in the presence of elders out of respect. As a matter of fact, *huqah* as an indulgence or a privilege was a great definer of etiquette (*tahzib*). No subject, however high he might have ranked in blood or royal favour, could presume to smoke *huqah* in the presence of the king or the reigning *nawab.* On state occasions it was offered to dignitaries considered equal in rank and therefore entitled to the privilege of smoking with him and the honour could not be refused even if they did not like to smoke. In that case, the *huqah-bardar* was asked to bring the *huqah* charged with the materials without the addition of fire. Application of the *munh-nal* (mouth-piece) to the mouth indicated the acceptance of the honour conferred. It was with this etiquette that the *huqah* was smoked in the royal household.

(c) Pan (Betel-leaf)

Tea had not been introduced in the age of the Great Mughals and *pan*-chewing was the most common practice. The Hindus had been using *pan* (*tambula*) since ancient times. Akbar's historian noted that though it was properly speaking a vegetable, connoisseurs called it an excellent fruit. Amir Khusrau ((1254-1325 A.D.) commented that it was an excellent fruit like the flower of a garden, and it was the finest fruit of Hindustan. It was, in fact, a leaf specifically prepared with several ingredients. The eating of the leaf rendered the breath agreeable and odorous. It strengthened the gums and made the hungry satisfied and the satisfied hungry.

It was grown on creepers and cultured with care. There were several species of pan-leaves popular during the medieval times, the choicest being *Bilhari*, *Kaker*, *Jaiswar*, *Kapuri*, *Kapurkant* (*Banarsi*) and *Banglah*. *Makhi* of Bihar and *Keroah* of Orissa were most favoured by the connoisseurs. Akbar's historian recorded that a bundle called *lahasa* contained 11,000 (110 x 100) leaves. Now it contains 14,000 (70 x 200) leaves. One bundle of 200 *pan* leaves was called *dholi*. In winter, they turned and arranged the leaves after four or five days; in summer every day. From 5 to 25 leaves, and sometimes more, were placed above each other and displayed in various ways.

Pan was specially prepared. Perfectly tempered liquid lime (*chuna*) was first pasted on betel-leaf. Then liquid catechu (*kattha*) prepared with milk and flavours was applied upon it. Then *supari* pieces (areca-nut) were placed on it and it was rolled and set with a clove (*laung*). Camphor, musk, saffron and other costly ingredients, and sometimes aphrodisiacs, were added to it. When tied by a silk thread, it was called *bira*. Gradually a large number of preparations were evolved and different types came into fashion. *Pan* preparation and service became a culture in itself, and *pan-dan* (container of *pan* and its ingredients) became an essential part, not only of the Mughal *harem*, but of every honourable household. *Bira* offered to a courtier by the king was a mark of royal favour which he received with the greatest courtesy. Normally too, *pan* was offered as a token of respect and goodwill, and was duly received with courtesy. All this developed into a pan-culture. *Pan*-chewing became the most popular practice. Though essentially an addiction, as it is, the Mughals made *pan* an institution and *pan*-service an etiquette, which has lasted to this day.

9

Medicines and Aphrodisiacal Drugs

Strict *purdah* was observed within the *harem* quarters and no male, howsoever important a functionary he could be, was allowed to enter it. Even the male *hakims* (physicians) were not allowed to go inside the palace and the stories recorded by some European travellers as to how the physicians among them were ushered in to examine the sick ladies and how lustfully did these sex-hungry human beings behave even behind the curtain, are all concocted. Like female painters and musicians, there were trained and experienced female *hakims* who were competent to deal with normal ailments. In case of exigency, they examined the sick lady and reported the symptoms to one of the court-*hakims* who waited outside the palace. He diagnosed the disease and prescribed the cure.

Mostly, indigenous vegetational and herbal medicines were used. These were prepared by the *hakims* themselves to ensure purity. Ingredients, and even some ready-made medicines, were also supplied by local *attars* (chemists; medical-men). Preparations from precious stones, metals and minerals were made with great care and cost, in accordance with the climatic and dietary conditions. These were effective and cured, and did not, in any way, affect the body adversely.

A female *jarrah* (surgeon) was also attached to the *Shafa'-Khanah* (hospital) of the palace who performed minor surgeries. Complicated diseases which now require major surgery, were then treated medically. These were cured in a large number of cases. The sick lady was not taken out of the palace even when medication failed and she required major surgery by a male *jarrah*. She eventually succumbed to her illness. Human life was not very precious during the medieval period. A slave-girl or a concubine could be replaced. They were there in the hundreds and were easily available. There was not much a loss even when a queen died, unless she was a Mumtaz Mahal. Only the life of the king mattered and it was most carefully guarded. Best *hakims* were engaged to keep him in good health and to cater to his physical needs.

A separate apartment was maintained in the palace for maternity. Old and experienced *dais* (mid-wives) were employed on a permanent basis to manage child-births which, in proportion to the population of the *harem* was a regular feature. Best and costliest medicines and diet were provided. Wet nurses (*dhay*) called *anaga* were engaged for breast-feeding. Every thing was meticulously organised, worked, and recorded. Efficiency was the watchword and there was no place for incompetent and insincere persons in the Mughal establishment.

The matters related to sex were, however, most precisely worked out. Ecstasy and bliss from sex was comparable to *Brahmananda*, of which this was the only phenomenon to give a glimpse and the Mughals too, like any other human being, loved to enjoy sex. Being the wealthiest people in the contemporary world, they could afford it in ways which were not accessible to others and were, in fact, incomprehensible to the contemporaries and are almost unintelligible to us today. Extraordinary was the composition of the Mughal *harem* where only a single male was to satisfy the physical needs of a large number of women. Fortunately, the *Kama-Shastras* (texts) on erotics of the ancient Hindus had detailed formulae and recipes of certain aphrodisiacal drugs which were prescribed to meet with such situations. Akbar, the founder of the Mughal system, had total faith in the country's intellectual legacy and he almost exclusively drew on indigenous sources in this respect, as he did in respect of dishes, perfumes and other things which went into the making of his life-pattern.

(a) Preliminary Medicines

The *Kama-Shastras* dealt with medicines and drugs on this subject in a separate *adhikarana* (section) which shows that the ancient people attached great importance to the treatment, preparation and acclimatisation of the human body for this purpose. A number of recipes were prescribed for bringing about the beauty of the face which was a primary condition of sex, e.g. a paste of *tagar, kuth* and leaves of *talish;* a paste of refined flour of barley, *mulahthi*, white *sarson* (mustard) and *lodh;* paste of leaves of *bad, kachnar, mahuwa, priyangu, kamal* (lotus), *sahdevi, harichandan, lakh, keshar* (saffron) and *pathani-lodh;* a paste of seed of plum-stone, skin of the root of bamboo, *shabarlodh* and yellow *sarson* (mustard) to be used in the winter season; a paste of the root of *kateri*, black *til*, skin of *daru-haldi* and *vitush-jaw*, a paste of the root of *kusha*, white *chandan* (sandalwood), *khas*, bark of *shirish*, *saunf* (aniseed) and *santhi*-rice, to be used in the spring season; a paste of *kumud*, *kamal*, *kahlar*, *dub*, *mulethi*, white *chandan* to be used in the summer season; and a paste of *agar*, *til*, *khas*, *balchhad*, *tagar and padmakashtha* to be used in the rainy season. The texts described some compositions for the removal of facial black spots and stains and some oils for softening and brightening of the skin.

The medieval people also used some preparations for dyeing the hair black. The following were the most important formulae:

(1) a mixture of powdered *madayantika* (*mehndi*), *kutaja* (*kuda*), *kavanjika*, *parvati-chameli* and *mashparni*, rubbed into the hair before bath;

(2) a special concoction prepared from oil of *guthli* (stone) of mango, powder of *kanta* stone, powder of *kakadani* fruits, powder of iron, and oil of *ankol;*

(3) a concoction prepared from seeds of *gunj*, *kuth*, *ela*, *devadaru* and juice of *bhangra;*

(4) a paste of burnt powder of ivory and juice of *bhangra* mixed with milk of goat;

(5) a concoction of *motha*, *sarson* (mustard), *usir*, *haritaki* and *amalaki;*

(6) a paste of powdered root of *nil*, *sendha salt* and small *pipal* (long pepper), mixed with *ghee* (clarified butter);

(7) a concoction of *morshikha*, juice of *bhangra* and *ghee* of cow;

(8) a paste of black *til*, juice of *gudhal* flowers and honey;

(9) a paste prepared from powdered *triphala* (*har, baheda* and *aonla*), iron, roots of *nili* and *bhrangi* mixed with urine of goat.

A number of medicines were used by the medieval people for the removal of unwanted hair from the body (e.g. pubic hair) to ensure cleanliness. These recipes were also prepared from *deshi* ingredients and were essentially Ayurvedic medicines. Hence there were absolutely no adverse after-effects. Some of the most important preparations were as follows:

(1) a concoction of powdered *harital, talbij, sindur, ghan-nad, kandali-ksar,* seeds of bitter *turai, vach, snuhimul, manjitha, varun* and *girikarna,* mixed and tempered first with milk of *snuhi* and then with juice of bitter *turai;*

(2) a paste of powder of burnt conchshell, burnt *dhak* (*palash*) wood and *harital* mixed with *kusum* oil;

(3) a concoction of powdered *bhujang* (*nagchurn*) and mustard-oil;

(4) a paste of powdered burnt *dhak* (*palash*) wood and *tal* mixed with juice of banana root;

(5) a mixture of *harital* and mustard oil, which had been tempered for seven days by sun-rays;

(6) a paste of burnt conchshell and powdered *harital* mixed with juice of banana;

(7) a paste of *harital* and burnt *palash* wood mixed with juice of banana.

Babur and Humayun had little facial hair owing to their Central Asian lineage. Both of them sported thin beard. Akbar shaved his beard and trimmed his moustache. So did Jehangir in his own style. Shah Jehan and Aurangzeb trimmed both their beards and moustaches. Expert and trustworthy barbers were employed in the imperial service for hair-cutting and keeping the facial hair in perfect order and style. Razor sharp *chhuras* (knives) were used for shaving.

Owing to certain natural secretions from the vaginal track, the female pudenda usually gave a bad, repulsive, pungent odour. The Mughals were very sensitive to odours and adequate means were adopted to examine and purify a woman before she was taken to the imperial bed. Normally, it was washed by boiled and saturated *neem* water which worked as an antiseptic and anti-bacterial medicine. Incense of *haldi* (turmeric), *ghee* (clarified butter), black *agar* (aloewood) and *gugal* was also used to remove its bad odour. Certain compositions (*yoga*) were also prescribed for internal and external application for this purpose, e.g.

(1) a concoction of *kuth, kamal* (lotus flower), *ilaichi* (cardamom) mixed with mustard oil;

(2) a concoction of *chameli* flowers, *mulethi*, flowers of mango, *jamun* (blackberry), *kaith, bijaura* and *bel* mixed with mustard oil;

(3) a concoction of *chameli* flowers and white *sarson* (mustard);

(4) powder of *vach, adusa*, bitter *parwal*, flowers of *priyangu* and leaves of neem;

(5) powder of *dalchini* (cinnamon), small *ilaichi* (cardamom), *tejpat, nagkeshar, kankol, laung* (clove), *agar* (aloewood) and *chharchhabila;*

(6) powder of dried flowers of *palash* (*dhak* or *taisu*), flowers of *dhay*, bark of *jamun* (blackberry), *manjith, mochrasa* and *ral;*

(7) a concoction of *devadaru*, black *til*, bark of *neem*, bark of

anar (pomegranate), flowers of *kamal* (lotus) and bark of *kachnar* mixed and adequately boiled in mustard oil.

Certain recipes were used for the contraction of vagina and this was the most important aspect of purification (*samskara*) of woman. The vaginal function was, in fact, the most dynamic aspect of human biology and every attempt was made to use it for the greatest sexual pleasure. Some of the most important pastes applied inside the *madan-mandir* (the temple of eros) for contracting it were as follows:

(1) a paste of fruits (seeds) of *tal-makhana* pounded in water;

(2) paste of powdered *mansil,* white pepper, *kahuakut,* gum of *kundru,* white *zira* (cuminseed), seeds of *talmakhana* and bark of the root of *kaith* mixed with honey;

(3) paste of powdered *babul* fruit, *mendhasingi* (horn of ram), *mansil* and *haldi* (turmeric) mixed with water;

(4) paste of powdered *pathani-lodh,* leaves of cotton, *haldi* (turmeric) and stone of plum mixed with honey;

(5) powder of *majuphal* (gallnut) *phitkari* (alum), skin of *anar* (pomegranate) fruit and *harad* (myrobalan);

(6) paste of powdered *saunth* (dry ginger), droppings of pigeon, *kahuakuth, hartal* and *sendha* salt with honey;

(7) powder of *haldi* (turmeric), *daru-haldi, kamal-keshar* (pollen-grain of lotus) and *devadaru;*

(8) paste of *dhay*-flowers, *triphala* (*har, baheda* and *aonla*), bark of *jamun* (blackberry) mixed with honey of large bee;

(9) paste of powdered *nilkamal, kutha, vach,* small *pipal* (long pepper), *ashwagandha, haldi* and *daru-haldi* mixed with water;

(10) paste of *manphal* and *kapur* (camphor) mixed with honey;

(11) powder of *vir-vadhuti* and *samkhpushpi;*

(12) powder of refined mercury, root of *bhupilu, pipal* (long pepper) and rice;

(13) paste of powdered *vach, nilophar* (blue lotus), *kutha, kalimirch* (black pepper), *asgandha* and *haldi* (turmeric) mixed with honey;

(14) paste of *manphal* and *kapur* (camphor) mixed with honey;

(15) paste of fruits of *palash* and *gular* pounded in *til*-oil and mixed with honey;

(16) The most frequently used paste, however, was prepared from *kamal* (lotus flower) along with its *nal* (stem) pounded in water or milk. It was as effective as it was simple. It also removed bad odour of the genitalia.

Simultaneously with the contraction (*sankochana*) of the female part, prescriptions were followed for the enlargement (*vardhana*) of the male organ. The texts dealt with this aspect too, in full details, and recorded the age-old and well-tried recipes. Some means prescribed by them were painful and did not suit the temperament (*mizaj*) of the Mughals. Wool (*rom*) of an insect called *jalshuk* was largely used in preparation of these medicines. It was thoroughly pounded and used with mustard oil. The most commonly used paste was prepared with root of *asgandha,* root of *lodh,* wool of *jalshuk,* fruit of large *kateri* and *hadjod,* mixed with *ghee* of buffalo. Other formulae of *jalshuk* were prepared with powdered *til, sarson* (mustard) and *saptaparna;*

vankarela, ral (bitumen) and juice of *kateri* fruits; *bhilawa,* onion, large flowers of *shal, kurahi,* lotus leaves, juice of *kateri* fruits and *gobar* (dung); *tejpat* and *ghee* of buffalo etc.

But it was a little poisonous and other safe compositions (*yoga*) were preferred. The most important of these were:

(1) paste of burnt *guthli* (stone) of *bhilawa,* leaves of lotus and *sendha* salt, mixed in the juice of the fruit of large *kateri;*

(2) paste of *guthli* (stone), of *bhilawa,* fruit of large *kateri,* leaves of lotus, *sendha* salt, mixed with *ghee* of buffalo, applied after the treatment of the organ by a mixture of *gobar* (dung) and root of *asgandha;*

(3) concoction of root of *asgandh,* root of large *lodh,* fruits of large *kateri, ghee* of buffalo, seed of *palash* (dhak), juice of *hadjod* mixed and specially prepared with mustard oil and milk;

(4) concoction of *asgandh, balchhad, kuth, jatamansi* and fruits of large *kateri* specially prepared with four times of mustard oil and four times of milk;

(5) a similar concoction prepared from *asgandh, saunth* (dried ginger), juice of *dhatura,* butter and *gobar* (dung);

(6) paste of *asgandh, kuth, jatamansi, savarkand* mixed with water;

(7) paste of *asgandh, vach, kuth, jatamansi* and white *sarson* (mustard) mixed with water;

(8) paste of yellow *sarson* (mustard), *tagar, kuth, talish,* fruits of *kateri* and *asgandh* mixed with milk of goat;

(9) paste of *hadjod, gudvach, asgandh, virvadhuti,* yellow fruits

of *kateri* mixed with warm water;

(10) paste of root of *babul*, seeds of *dhatura, asgandh, virvadhuti*, yellow fruits of *kateri* mixed with milk of goat;

(11) powder of root of white *kaner*, root of *apamarg*, root of *asgandh*, root of *kalihari* and seeds of *kateri;*

(12) paste of *sendha* salt, *marich, kuth, brahati, kharmanjari, asgandh* (*ashwagandha*), *jau, mash, pipal,* white *sarson (*mustard), white *til* mixed with honey;

(13) paste of powdered *nagvala* (*gangren*), *khirenti, vach, ashwagandha, gajpipal,* root of white *kaner* mixed with butter;

(14) paste of seeds of pomegranate and *balamkhira, elua,* juice of *kateri* fruits mixed with mustard oil;

(15) paste of juice of *chameli* leaves, *manshil, kuth, saunth, kali mirch* (black pepper), *pipal* (long pepper), *suhaga* (borax) mixed with *til*-oil.

There was absolutely no need to use contraceptives during the medieval period. It is entirely a modern phenomenon.

(b) Aphrodisiacal Drugs: *Dravana*

The texts discussed various means of *Vashikarana* (enslavement of women), e.g. by presentation of flowers and perfumes; clothes and ornaments; grants and other things in fulfilment of their desires. The Mughals did not believe in the tantric means prescribed by the texts, otherwise, all this was very simple for them and they could very well afford to follow these means as a routine. Over and above these, they adopted a number of aphrodisiacal drugs prescribed by the texts. These can be classed into four categories in accordance with their subjects and functions. *Dravana* was the first class. Medicines under this class were prepared for application either inside the vagina or upon the phallus before coitus. Their application hastened female orgasm and brought about excessive pleasure on the part of the woman only by a little effort by the man. These are described in the texts under *vashikarana* because their use enslaved women. The following were the most important formulae of the *dravana* class:

(1) Equal quantities of *saunth* (dry ginger), *kali-mirch* (black pepper) and *pipal* (long pepper) were powdered and mixed with honey of large bee. The paste was applied inside the vagina in a safe quantity.

(2) Purified *parad* (mercury) extracted form *hingul* (cinnabar) was mixed with the juice of *chameli* leaves and the paste was applied inside the vagina. It must be noted that, though effective, mercury was a harmful ingredient and it was used extremely cautiously.

(3) Powder of *imli* (tamarind) seeds and *sindur* (cinnabar) were mixed equally with honey of small bee. The paste was applied inside the vagina in a safe quantity.

(4) *Kapur* (camphor), burnt *suhaga* (borax) and purified *parad* (mercury) obtained from *hingul* (cinnabar) were powdered and mixed in equal quantities with honey of small bee. The paste was applied upon the phallus in a safe quantity. It was allowed to remain there for some time and dry, then it was cleaned by a cloth just before coitus.

(5) Burnt *suhaga* (borax) and juice of *agastya* leaves were mixed with honey and *ghee* and the paste was applied on the phallus in safe quantity.

(6) Powdered seeds of *imli* (tamarind), *saunth* (dry ginger), *kali-mirch* (black pepper) and *pipal* (long pepper) were mixed with old *gud* (jaggery) and honey and applied in safe quantity on the phallus.

(7) Powdered *kali-mirch* (black pepper), seeds of *dhatura* (thorn apple; belladonna) and *pipal-lodh* (yellow long pepper) were mixed with honey and applied on the phallus two hours before coitus.

(8) Pieces of *thor* (*thuhar*) were pasted in adequate quantities with *manahshila* (*menshil*) and *gandhak* (sulphur) and perfectly dried. These were powdered and mixed with honey. The paste was applied on the phallus two hours before coitus.

Other pastes of the *dravana* category, for application on phallus, had the following ingredients:

(9) fine powder of *kadamba* leaves mixed with honey;

(10) powdered *sendha* salt, *piplamul* and *mulethi* mixed with the juice of *kaith;*

(11) powdered seeds of *lajjalu, mulethi* and *kuth* mixed with honey;

(12) powdered *ghudvach, jaljamani, bakuchi, juhi*-flower, rose-flower and *vrishchakali* mixed with honey;

(13) powder of *indra-jan, pathani-lodh, khas, manjith* and white mustard mixed with honey;

(14) powder of the gum of *kaner,* small *pipal* (long pepper) and rice mixed with honey;

(15) powdered small *pipal* (long pepper), rice, *gokharu* and *kateri*-fruit, mixed with honey;

(16) dried and powdered flowers of yellow *juhi* and *kadamba*

fruit, mixed with honey;

(17) paste of *sendha* salt and pigeon droppings mixed with honey; this formula was very frequently used by the common people;

(18) powdered *gorochan, kapur* (camphor) *parad* (mercury), *keshar* (saffron) and *chandan* (sandalwood) mixed with the juice of *dhatura* (belladonna);

(19) paste of gum of *malshri* and purified mercury mixed with honey; purified mercury can also be used with juice of *gangren* or juice of *sahdevi* with the same effect;

(20) paste of *kapur* (camphor) with burnt *suhaga* (borax) and mercury mixed with honey;

(21) mercury can also be used with *gud* (jaggery) and *imli* (tamarind);

(22) paste of old *gud* (jaggery), seeds of *imli* (tamarind) and bitter *turai* mixed with honey.

(c) *Stambhana* Drugs

The medicines under this class, used by man on various parts of his body, delayed (sometimes indefinitely) male ejaculation, creating excessive sexual pleasure to both the participants in the act of coitus. The following were the most important prescriptions of the *stambhana* class:

(1) Seeds of *lajjawanti* were pounded in the milk of cow and milk (juice) of *thuhar.* If the man applied this paste profusely on his legs before coitus it greatly delayed ejaculation.

(2) Powder of the root of *santhi* was mixed with the oil of *kusumbha.* This was applied on the soles of a man's feet before coitus, for *stambhana.*

(3) Root and flower of *makoy* and *paragkaisar* (pollen grain) of white lotus were powdered and mixed with honey of small bee. This paste was profusely applied on the man's navel (*nabhi*) before coitus. This ensured *stambhana*.

(4) Bark of *shisham* tree, purified *parad* (mercury) extracted from *hingul* (cinnabar) and *kapur* (camphor) were pounded in equal quantities and mixed with honey. This paste if applied on the navel of the man ensured *stambhana*.

(5) When a man engaged in coitus keeping seeds of *amaltas* in his mouth, ejaculation was indefinitely delayed.

(6) Seeds of *tal-makhana* bearing white flowers were pounded with milk of *bud*. This paste was placed in the seeds of *kanja*. If a man engaged in the sexual act keeping these *kanja* seeds in his mouth, he could control ejaculation.

(7) Juice of *kanja* leaves applied on soles and palms was also effective.

(8) Juice of leaves of black *dhatura* applied on soles also helped.

(9) Paste of *kaisar* (pollen grain) of *kateri*, *kapur* (camphor) and honey was dried and reduced into small balls of the size of *zira* (cuminseed). If a man engaged in coitus keeping one such piece in his mouth it brought about *stambhana*.

(10) Ejaculation was also delayed if he kept root of *kaunch* of the size of a finger in his mouth during the sexual act.

(11) A simple formula of a mixture of milk of goat and camel and *ghee* of cow, applied on legs was also effective and popularly used by the people owing to simple, easily available ingredients.

(12) A powder of *akarkara*, *saunth*, *kankol*, *keshar* (saffron),

pipal (long pepper), *jayphal* (nutmeg), *laung* (clove), white *chandan* (sandalwood) and opium was prepared and eaten daily with honey in safe quantity for a fortnight. It ensured excessive sexual pleasure along with *stambhana*. It is noteworthy that only a few medicines were prescribed for oral use and almost all of them (for oral use) contained opium, which was a little harmful.

Scores of other formulae of *stambhana* were followed. Recipes with different compositions were prescribed because the contexts varied from person to person and season to season. One could choose the best one, in accordance with his physiology, nature and temperament (*mizaj*).

A man could meet several women the same night if he applied a *stambhana* prescription upon himself and a *dravana* prescription upon the women. This combination, in fact, much facilitated the task of the polygamous Mughals.

(d) *Vajikarana* Drugs

The texts enjoined that the use of the prescriptions under this class enabled the man to perform the sexual act with the vigour of a horse, hence its nomenclature: *vajikarana* (the making of the horse). These medicines which were eaten or drunk (in contrast to the *dravana* and *stambhana* drugs which were, mostly externally applied) brought about extraordinary sexual strength and virility among males. He could copulate satisfactorily with 10, 20 or even 100 women at a time, as the texts affirmed, and by virtue of their nature and the prevailing circumstances, these were most favoured by the Mughals. Some of the important formulae of this class were as follows:

(1) A concoction of *utankan* (*uchchata*) and *mulethi* (*murahati*)

taken with milk gave extraordinary virility to the man.

(2) Powdered *mulethi* mixed with *ghee* (clarified butter) and honey and taken with milk of cow, gave the same effect.

(3) Milk in which testes, either of a he-goat or ram, were boiled and mixed with sugar was also used for *vajikarana*.

(4) Testes of the he-goat were boiled in milk. These were then fried in *ghee* and mixed with small *pipal* (long pepper) and salt. The man who ate this preparation could copulate with 100 women. The residue milk mixed with black *til* was equally effective.

(5) Powder of *bidarikand*, *vanslochan* and seeds of *kaunch* was drunk with milk of cow for the same purpose.

(6) A drink of *bidarikand*, *ghee* and milk was a *vajikarana*. This herb was also used with other ingredients for this purpose.

(7) Powdered seeds of *kaunch* and *tal-makhana* drunk with milk of cow gave extraordinary virility to man.

(8) This drink could also be made with *vanslochan*, instead of *kaunch*.

(9) Powder of *chiraunji*, *muhar* (*morta* or *murahari*) and white *bidarikand* was taken with milk for ten to fifteen days regularly, for this purpose.

(10) Concoction of *singhara*, *kaseru*, fruits of *mahuwa*, *ksirkakoli* milk and sugar prepared with *ghee* on light heat made a man capable of copulating with numerous women.

(11) *Khir* (sweet curry) prepared with de-skinned pulse of *urad* fried in *ghee* and milk of cow was the most popular *vajikarana* used by the people. Powder of fried *urad* was also taken with *ghee*, honey and milk. The texts enjoined that these preparations of *urad* enable even an old man to act as a sixteen-year-old boy.

(12) *Khir* prepared with rice and eggs of *chatak* (sparrow bird) and *ghee* and honey was also used for this purpose. Eggs of *chatak* were also used with several other ingredients with the same effect.

(13) A preparation was made with *ghee*, honey, sugar, *mulethi*, *mulahri* and milk.

(14) *Shatavari, gokharu, pipal* (long pepper), honey, *ghee* of goat and milk of cow were used in another *vajikarana* preparation. *Gokharu* was also used with *jau* (barley) in other compositions.

(15) Powdered *nagauri-asgandh, bhidayra, mishri* (sugarcandy) were taken with milk.

(16) Powdered *aonla,* specially prepared in its own juice, was effectively used with honey and milk.

A large number of other prescriptions, all invariably being compositions of various herbs, precisely vegetational medicines, were used for *vajikarana* during the medieval period. A *hakim* at Agra still prepares these recipes and the tradition of this medical science is still alive.

(e) *Auparishtaka* Means

Such works as Chanakya's *Arthashastra* were known and read, and their precepts were followed by Akbar. The system of spying inside the King's own palace by trusted female spies was organised effectively in accordance with the instructions of these ancient texts. These were repositories of centuries of experience and knowledge, and he reposed faith in them.

These texts prescribed the use of *Auparishtakas,* or artificial means to satisfy female urge in case of a polygamous king whose virility was impaired on account of old age or over-indulgence. The

sheer number of women in the *harem* also required the use of such devices. The stories recorded by foreign travellers that the ladies used cucumber (*khira, kakadi*) or such similar vegetables are, however, concocted and untrue. There was no need to take recourse to such lowly means. These were not unprecedented situations and the texts discussed the artificial means under the heading *Auparishtaka* in full details, not only as theoretical formulae but for actual use in such circumstances.

These were artificial phalluses (phalli) of exact form and size of the natural ones made of gold, silver, copper, iron, ivory, horn of cow and wood, in that order. These were, mostly, hollow and smooth, bearing a number of small nodules on its front end to enhance the woman's coital pleasure. These were either attached to the waist to be free to function like a real phallus or used separately. That several types of *apadravyas*, as these were specifically termed, evolved gradually shows that these artificial membra were in usage in the Raniwas of the ancient Hindu, and *harem* of the medieval, kings with or without the knowledge of the lord of the household. Lesbian women were largely tempted to use these means.

10

Mughal Amusements and Pastimes

The ladies of the Mughal *harem* did not cook, or sweep floors, or wash clothes, or prepare lights. They did not even bring up children. All this work was done by maid-servants and slave-girls who were specially trained for each work. How did then, they pass their time, day in and day out, confined within the walls of the *harem* as they were?

(a) Functions and Ceremonies

Special functions and ceremonies were organised on important occasions during the year. Akbar instituted the celebration of *Nauroz* or the New Year's Day when the sun entered Aries. It lasted till the nineteenth day of the month (*Farwardin* of the *Ilahi* era). Two days of this period were considered great festivals when much money and numerous other things were distributed as presents, viz. the first day and the nineteenth day. Following the custom of the ancient Parsis, banquets were also held on 3rd *Urdibihisht*, 6th *Khurdad*, 13th *Tir*, 7th *Amurdad*, 4th *Shahriwar*, 16th *Mihr*, 10th *Aban*, 9th *Azar*, 8th, 15th and 23rd *day*, 2nd *Bahman* and 5th *Isfandarmuz*. Feasts were held on these days and people rejoiced. The whole *harem* was engaged in the celebrations. *Naqqaras* were beaten and coloured lamps were lighted.

Birthdays were similarly very pompously celebrated. The ceremony of weighing, viz. *tula-dan*, which was essentially a Hindu custom was instituted by Akbar and was scrupulously followed by his successors, including the puritan and orthodox Aurangzeb. It was held twice a year. On the first day of the month of *Aban* (15th October) which was the solar anniversary of Akbar, he was weighed twelve times against gold, quick-silver, silk, perfumes, copper, *ruh-i-tutiya*, drugs, *ghee*, iron, rice-milk, seven kinds of grain and salt. According to the number of years he had lived, there was given away an equal number of sheep, goats and fowls to the people who bred these animals. A great number of small animals were also set free. He was weighed a second time on the 5th of Rajab, his lunar birthday, against eight articles: silver, tin, cloth, lead, fruits, mustard-oil and vegetables. On both occasions, the festival of *sal-girih* (birthday) was celebrated with much gaiety and enthusiam, and the whole *harem* was engaged in it. There was a *jashn* or feast which was of special importance for the *harem*. The articles against which the royal person was weighed were sent from the *harem*, or by the mother of the reigning emperor. Jehangir has recorded to have been weighed in the palace of his mother. It was, in fact, in the *harem* that the string with as many knots as the emperor had numbered years was kept.

The princes, sons and grandsons of His Majesty, were weighed once in every solar year. They were for the first time weighed when two years old, but only against one thing. Every year, however, an additional thing was put on the scales. When grown up they were generally weighed against seven or eight things but not against more than twelve. Animals were set free as usual. A separate treasurer and an accountant were appointed and the expenditure of the department of *tula-dan* was carefully recorded.

Occasions of circumcision of the princes and marriages of princes and princesses were celebrated with great gusto and provided engagement to the *harem* inmates. Some Muslim festivals like *Id* and *Shab-e-Barat* and Hindu festivals such as *Rakhi*, *Diwali* and *Holi* were also celebrated in the Mughal *harem*, and provided the ladies a much-needed change from the daily routine.

(b) *Mina Bazar*

Akbar instituted the *Khush-Roz* (The Happy Day) or the Day of the Fancy Bazar (*Mina Bazar*) on the third feast day of every month. A *bazar* (market) exclusively for the ladies was held. The merchants of the age brought articles from all countries. The ladies of the *harem* and other women attended it and there was brisk buying and selling. The king used such days to select articles which he liked and also fixed prices of the things. He utilised this occasion also to scrutinise the affairs of the *harem* people, and to arrange marriages of boys and girls. To such days, he gave the name of *Khush-Roz* or the joyful day, as they were a source of much enjoyment.

After the fancy *bazars* for women, *bazars* for men were also held where merchants of all countries sold their wares. The king watched the transactions. The *bazar* people, on such occasions, laid their grievances before him, without being prevented by the mace-bearers and also used the opportunity of laying out their stores in order to explain their circumstances. A separate treasurer and accountant were attached also to this department.

The buildings of these two *bazars* are still there at Fatehpur Sikri: the men's *bazar* is situated south of the Mahal-i-Ilahi (so-called Birbal's Palace) and is at present erroneously known as 'Horses' Stables' (pl. 16). The *Mina Bazar* or women's fancy *bazar* is situated east of it, just attached to the western wall of the Raniwas (so-called, Jodhbai's Palace) and is most absurdly called 'Camels' Stables'. It is adequately enclosed and covered and the whole of it has been architecturally planned to ensure seclusion and *purdah*. Shops are distinctly demarcated in it.

16. Shahi-Bazar, Fatehpur Sikri

Mina Bazar was held by his successors also. Jehangir is recorded to have held *Mina Bazar* inside the fort (of Agra) at night. It was a private affair, exclusive to the ladies of the *harem*, around which many a romantic tale was woven. Like a village hat or painth, it was a weekly fair and the surprising feature is that it was held regularly in tents even when the king was travelling and living in camp. Shah Jehan continued to follow the custom. This is how it was institutionalised. Certainly it provided an occasion to the ladies to purchase cloths, ornaments, cosmetics and other things of their daily need and to while away the time in shopping.

(c) Amusements (Indoor Games)

Some time of the *harem* ladies, particularly of the elderly ones, was of course devoted to religious worship, adequate provision for which had been made within the *harem* precincts. But there was a limit to it in all social milieus in all ages, and certain forms of pastimes and amusements for these secluded human beings were needed as a matter of course. They could while away some time in *huqah*-smoking and *pan*-chewing, bathing and swimming in *harem* pools, gardening and such other innocent pastimes.

Story-telling and *gap-bazi* (gossiping), in the spirit of light conversation was also a pastime. Jehangir is recorded to have freely indulged in it. He had in his service a professional reciter and storyteller named Mulla Asad, who entertained the king by his gossips. The king liked his company and bestowed the title, *Mahfuz Khan* upon him. He was also rewarded with an elephant, a horse, a palanquin, a dress of honour and cash award of 1000 rupees. Once he was so pleased with him that the storyteller was weighed against rupees and the weight came up to 4400 rupees (which sum was given to him as a rule) and his *mansab* (rank) was raised to 200 *zat* (personal) and 20 *sawar* (horsemen). He was ordered 'always to be present at the meetings (of course in the *Ghusl-Khanah*) for

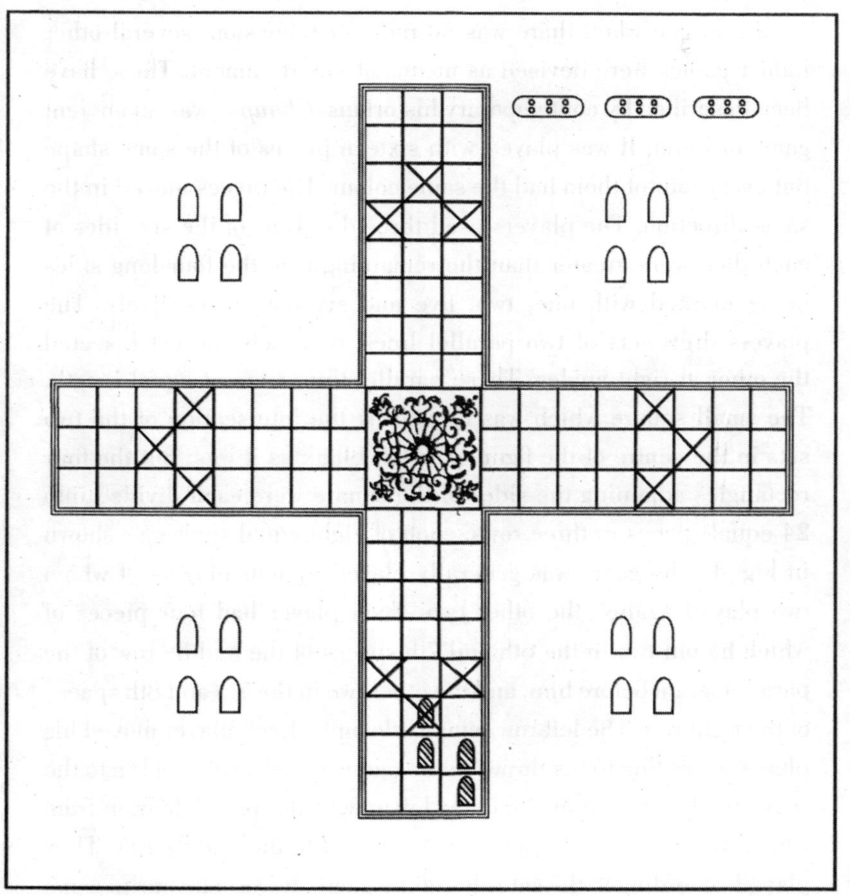

Fig. 4. Chaupar

talk (*gap-bazi*)' in the evenings. He was not like an English clown or court-jester, nor a *vidushak* of the Sanskrit plays, but a personal friend who entertained the emperor with grace and dignity, conducive to the Mughal etiquette. But his only function was to entertain the king by storytelling or *gap*. Women storytellers were similarly employed in the *harem* and they entertained the ladies by their light conversation. Puppet shows exclusively managed by women were also arranged for the entertainment of the *harem* inmates.

In an age when there was no radio or television, several other indoor games were devised as means of entertainment. These have been described by contemporary historians. *Chaupar* was an ancient game of India. It was played with sixteen pieces of the same shape but every four of them had the same colour. The pieces moved in the same direction. The players used three die. Four of the six sides of each dice were greater than the remaining two, the four long sides being marked with one, two, five and six dots respectively. The players drew sets of two parallel lines, of which one set bisected the other at right angles. These parallel lines were of equal length. The small square which was formed by the intersection of the two sets in the centre of the figure was left blank as it was; but the four rectangles adjoining the sides of the square were each divided into 24 equal spaces in three rows, each of eight equal spaces as shown in Fig. 4. The game was generally played by four players of whom two played against the other two. Each player had four pieces of which he put two in the 6th and 7th spaces of the middle row of the parallelogram before him, and the other two in the 7th and 8th spaces of the right row. The left row remained empty. Each player moved his pieces according to his throw, in the outer row, always keeping to the right, till he arrived at the outer left row of the parallelogram from which he started; and from there he moved to the middle row. They played according to the set rules of the game. It was a favourite game of the *harem* ladies and Zeb-un-Nissa, eldest daughter of Aurangzeb is recorded to have spent most of her time playing *chaupar* with her girl friends.

Akbar invented another indoor game which he named *chandal-mandal*. Its figure or board consisted of 16 parallelograms, arranged in a circular form round the centre. Each parallelogram was divided into 24 fields, every eight of which formed a row (Fig. 5). The number of pieces was 64. Four die were used, of which the four longer sides were marked with one, two, ten and twelve points respectively. The

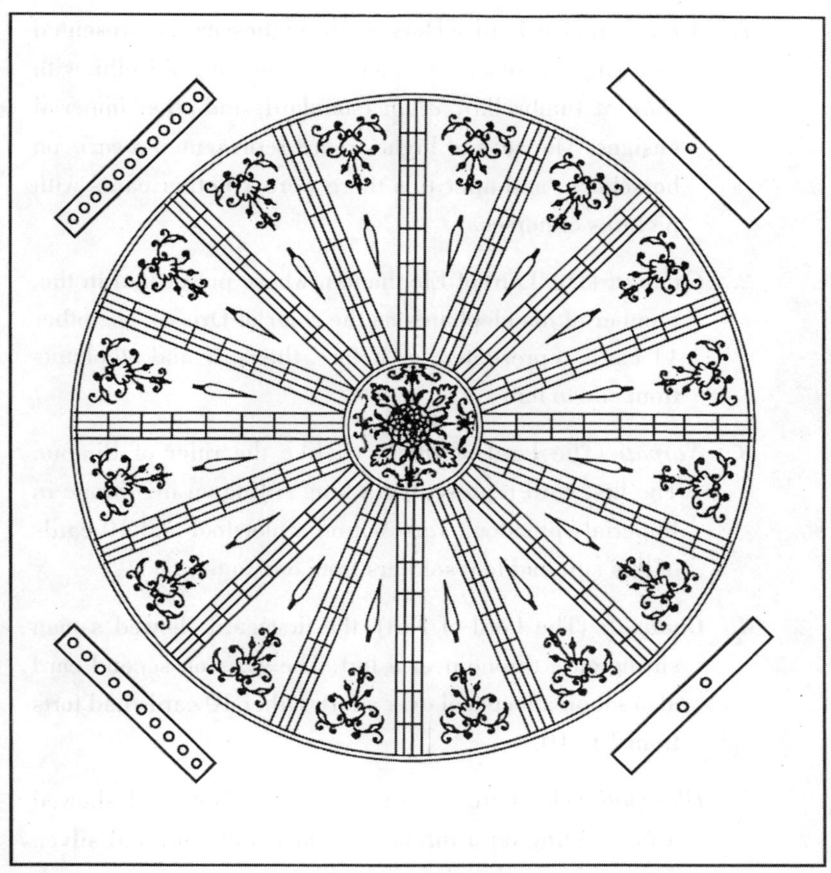

Fig. 5. Chandal Mandal

number of players was 16. Each got four pieces which were placed in the middle. As in *chaupar*, the pieces were moved to the right and passed through the whole circle. It was played in several ways. Akbar sometimes played it like chess (*shatranj*).

Playing cards or *ganjifa* was a well-known indoor game. Number 12 was its basis and it was divided into twelve categories each of 12 cards, there thus being 144 cards as follows:

1. *Ashwapati* (The Lord of Horses), the highest card represented by a king on horseback resembling the king of Delhi, with *chhatra* (umbrella), *'alam* (standard) and other imperial ensigns. The second highest card represented a *vazir* on horseback; and after this there were 10 other cards with pictures of horses.

2. *Gajapati* (The Lord of Elephants), whose power laid in the, number of his elephants as the ruler of Orissa. The other 11 cards represented, as before, the *vazir* and elephants from one to ten.

3. *Narpati* (The Lord of Infantry), like the ruler of Bijapur. The first card represented a king sitting on his throne in Imperial splendour. *Vazir* sat on a footstool and 10 cards of this suit had foot soldiers from one to ten.

4. *Gadhpati* (The Lord of Fort), the first card showed a man sitting on a throne over a fort. The *vazir* on second card also sat on a footstool over a fort. Other 10 cards had forts from 1 to 10.

5. *Dhanpati* (The Lord of Treasures), the first card showed a man sitting on a throne with heaps of gold and silver. The *vazir* was also shown amidst treasures on a footstool. Other 10 cards represented jars full of gold and silver from 1 to 10.

6. *Dalpati* (The Lord of Battle), the first card showed a king in armour sitting on his throne and surrounded by warriors with coats of mail. The *vazir* was also shown wearing breast armour. Ten other cards showed individuals clad in armour.

7. *Nawapati* (The Lord of Fleet), the first card showed a

man sitting on a throne in a ship. The *vazir* also sat on a footstool in a ship. Other 10 cards had boats from 1 to 10.

8. *Tiyapati* (The Queen of Ladies), who was shown on the first card sitting on a throne surrounded by her maids. The second card showed a woman as *vazir* on a footstool and the other 10 cards had pictures of women from 1 to 10.

9. *Surapati* (The Lord of Divinities) called Indra was shown on a throne on the first card. The *vazir* on the second card sat on a footstool. Ten other cards had pictures of divinities from 1 to 10.

10. *Asrpati* (The Lord of Genii), the first card represented Sulaiman, son of Daud on the throne. The *vazir* sat on a footstool and 10 other cards had genii.

11. *Banpati* (The Lord of Wild Beasts), the first card represented a tiger with some other animals. A leopard was shown as *vazir* on the second card. Ten other cards had pictures of wild beasts, as usual, from 1 to 10.

12. *Ahipati* (The Lord of Snakes), where the first card showed a serpent mounted on a dragon whilst the *vazir* was a serpent on another serpent of the same kind. The remaining ten cards showed serpents from 1 to 10.

Akbar made suitable alterations in the pictures of these cards in accordance with the composition of his various departments and it was in this subtle way that the game was played.

Chess (*shatranj*) was an ancient game of the Hindus which was also very popular with the Mughals. It was divided into 64 squares, eight on each of the four sides of the board. There were sixteen *muhras* (figures) on either side consisting of the king, his *vazir*, two horses (for left and right movement), two elephants, two camels and eight *piyadas* (foot-soldiers) each having its own rule of movement (Fig. 6). The game was played both two-handed and four-handed. Though Akbar was an expert player, he detested it owing to the great time the game consumed. However, it was deemed to be an imperial (*shahi*) game which called for wisdom and higher intellect, and was

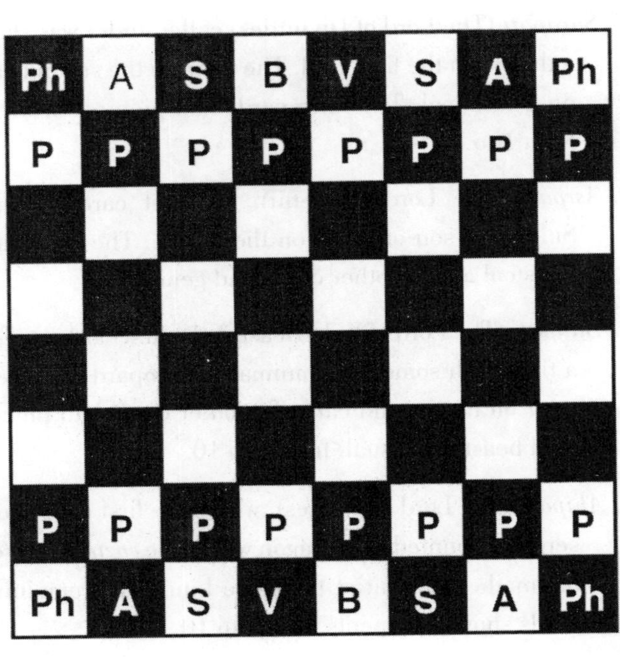

Fig. 6. Chess (Shatranj) Board

held in the highest esteem among indoor games. Jehangir and Shah Jehan used to play it with their queen-consorts. It was most popularly played in the Mughal *harem*, and a wide variety of *muhras* (figures) of ivory, sandalwood, silver and gold were in usage.

That Akbar played the game of chess with slave-girls as pieces moving on the chequered pavement of the *Pachisi* court at Fatehpur Sikri is a myth which was coined and circulated by over-zealous guides just to romanticise Mughal history. We have fantastic notions of medieval despots and we think that they were capable of any brutality. The *Chaupar* has been paved in the court (pl. 17) not for actual use but just as a specimen of the game for the knowledge of the people, particularly of the visitors from foreign lands and, of course, for posterity.

(d) Cultural, Artistic and Playful Engagements

Though the wardrobe was a separate department, the ladies of the *harem* also engaged themselves in embroidery, sewing and dress-making as a useful pastime. Some devoted themselves to practising

17. 'Chaupar' paved in the court, Fatehpur Sikri

calligraphy and copying the *Quran* which was considered to be a religiously meritorious engagement. Books of poetry and folklore were available in the *Shahi Kutubkhanah* (the imperial library which was a large establishment containing, during Akbar's reign, 25,000 books, same of which were illustrated), and these were requisitioned for reading in the *harem*. The ladies were adequately educated and had a literary taste. Some princesses were fond of composing verses, a number of them under the pen-name of *makhfi* (concealed), concealed within the *harem* walls as they really were. This way they could express their suppressed feelings and derived consolation. Poetry-writing and reciting, in fact, provided the ladies a sophisticated pastime. Instrumental music was another artistic engagement. *Dilruba* was the most favourite instrument. Many a legendery song of grief and sorrow were played and enjoyed. They soothed the soul: ('Our sweetest songs are those that tell of saddest thought'), and helped the inmates to reconcile with their circumstances. Painting was another fine art which provided the ladies with much needed respite.

This is the way we view the medieval *harem* today. We think they lived a miserable life and suffered by monotony but, obviously, our point of view is determined by modern notions of liberty and equality and is biased. The English lady who lived in the *zenanah* for twelve years has left a valuable record of her observations on the life of the *harem* ladies. She noted that at first she pitied the apparent monotony of their lives but this feeling was worn away as she lived intimately with them who were precluded from mixing generally with the world. They were happy in their confinement and never having felt the sweets of liberty, did not know how to use the boon if it were to be granted to them. As the bird from the nest immured in a cage was both cheerful and contented, so were these females. Truly, they did not have many intellectual resources, but they certainly had naturally good understanding, and having learned their duty they strived to fulfil it. So far as she had had any opportunity of making personal observations on their general character, they appeared to her as obedient wives, dutiful daughters, affectionate mothers, kind mistresses, sincere friends and liberal benefactresses to the distressed poor. These were their moral qualifications, and in their religious duties, they were zealous in performing the several ordinances which they had been instructed by their parents or husbands to observe. The customs were similarly honoured. If there was any merit in obeying the injunctions of their law-givers, those whom she had known most intimately deserved praise since they were faithful in what they professed.

The English lady further noted that to the ladies of the *harem* who were accustomed from infancy to confinement, this kind of life was by no means irksome. They had their employment, engagements and amusements, and though these were not exactly to modern tastes nor suited to modern mode of education, they were not the less relished by those for whom they were invented. They perhaps wondered equally at some of the English modes of dissipating time and fancied that the English ladies might have spent it more profitably. Be that as it may, the Muslim ladies with whom she had been long intimate appeared to her always happy, contented and satisfied with the seclusion to which they were destined; they desired no other and the English lady ceased to regret they could not be made partakers of that freedom of intercourse with the world, modern ladies deemed so essential to their happiness, since their health suffered nothing from that confinement by which they were preserved from a variety of snares and temptations. Besides this they deemed disgraceful in the highest degree to mix indiscriminately with men who were not relations. They were educated from infancy for retirement and they could have no wish that the custom could be changed which kept them apart from the society of men who were not related to them. Female society was unlimited and they enjoyed without restraint.

These females who were always very conscious for the character and honour of their house secluded themselves from the eyes of strangers, carefully instructing their young daughters to a rigid observance of their own prudent example. Little girls when four years old were kept strictly behind the *purdah* and if they moved out, it was always in covered conveyances, and under the guardianship of a faithful female domestic maid who was equally tenacious as the mother to preserve the young lady's reputation unblemished by concealing her from the gaze of men.

The ladies of the *zenanah* were not restricted from the society of their own sex. They were extravagantly fond of company and equally as hospitable when entertained. To be alone and solitary was a trial to which, in fact, they were seldom exposed. Every lady had companions amongst her dependents and according to her means the number in her establishment was regulated. Some ladies of rank had from two to ten companions, independent of slaves and domestic maids and there were some of the royal family who entertained in their service 200 or 300 female dependents of all classes. A well-filled *zenanah* was a mark of gentility and status. This narrative shows that they did not live as miserable a life as we think from our modern point of view. Medieval contexts cannot be judged through the perspectives of the present age.

The Mughal emperors were very fond of hunting and a separate department was maintained to manage it. Jehangir was most devoted to it. He allowed his queens, e.g. Nur Jehan Begum, to accompany him on such expeditions and even to shoot animals. The chief queens thus got ample opportunities to go out on excursions. The ladies of the *harem* were also allowed to sit behind curtains and watch animal-fights which were regularly held. This was a popular form of medieval entertainment. Akbar's historian has also described pigeon-flying (called *Ishq-Bazi*) as an amusement. Akbar was very fond of it and a department was created for its maintenance too. Pigeon-flying was also a *harem* pastime.

Perhaps the best companions of these caged human beings were the traditional innocent caged birds, viz. *shuk* and *sarika* (popularly, though erroneously, called *tota* and *maina*). These were ancient birds of India which could speak like human beings and talk; they could learn and repeat anything. Amir Khusrau noted that *shuka* (*tota*) was not like *tuti* (of Iran). It talked like human beings and exactly repeated whatever it heard. It could read the verses of the *Quran* (as fluently as Sanskrit *slokas*) and could offer prayer to God as it was taught. It could talk to the people as they talked among themselves. *Sharak*, which was a bird of the parrot species, small in size than *shuk*, spoke more distinctly and fluently. There was no obstacle in its speech. It could pronounce any word distinctly and correctly and there was no ambiguity in its speech. Both these birds had wonderful memory. Ladies used to keep these birds for companionship in India from ancient times, and Sanskrit plays are replete with their references. Babur has also referred to a wide variety of *sharaks* in his *Memoirs* and noted that not only could they speak whatever they had been taught, but also from their own heads. He was amazed and remarked that so long a person did not hear with his own ears, he could not believe. These were the best friends of the ladies of the Mughal *harem* who whiled away their time with them. They were kept in beautiful spacious cages of brass, copper, silver and, some times, gold wires and carefully fed and nursed. The ladies conversed with them intimately as if they were confidants, and taught them poems, verses and novelties which they repeated to their delight and recreation. These caged birds were, in fact, their best companions to whom they could freely express their feelings.

11

Illumination (Lighting) of the Mughal Palace

In the medieval period, when there were no match-boxes and no lighters, a permanent source of fire was made in the imperial household. It was a simple matter. At noon of the day when the sun entered the 19th degree of Aries, and the heat was maximum, the servants exposed to the rays of the sun a round piece of white and shining stone which was called *surajkrant*. A piece of cotton was then held near it, which caught fire from the heat of the stone. This celestial fire was preserved in a vessel called *agingir* (fire-pot) and committed to the care of an officer. The lamp-lighters, torch-bearers and cooks of the palace used this fire, which was renewed every year.

As soon as the sun set, the attendants of the palace lighted twelve white scented candles called *kafuri-shama'ha* (camphor candles) on twelve candlesticks of gold and silver and brought them before the king. A singer of sweet melodies with a candle in his hand sang a variety of delightful *ragas* (musical notes) to the praise of God, beginning and concluding with a prayer for the continuance of the auspicious reign. The whole palace was then lighted. This was the daily ritual.

A large number of beautiful candlesticks and shades of various forms and designs were used in the palace (Fig. 7). These were made by expert workmen in a separate department (*karkhanah;* every Mughal department where anything was produced was called *karkhanah* and there were about a hundred Mughal *karkhanas*). Some candlesticks weighed ten *mans* (each *man* was equal to 2160 *tolas* or 25.2 kilograms) and upwards. They were of various ingenious designs and were placed in broad round trays. Some were single, while others had two branches and more. Akbar invented a candlestick one yard high. Five others were placed on its top. Each was adorned with the figure of an animal. White wax candles, three yards and more in length were cast on it so that a ladder was required to snuff and light it.

Various types of *mashalas* (flambeaux or torches) and *diyas* (*dipas* or *dipakas* = small concave bowls), besides the candles, were also used in the palace for lighting. Mustard-oil was used in them. Some *diyas* contained oil and wicks (*battis*), while *binaulas* (cottonseeds) and oil were used in others (Fig 8). An interesting system prevailed. On the first, second and third nights of every lunar month when moonlight was there only for a short time, 8 wicks in each *diya* were lighted. A large number of *diyas* were placed in niches (*ale* or *taq*) made on the walls for this very purpose. Interconnecting corridors and passages were specifically illuminated. Wicks decreased in

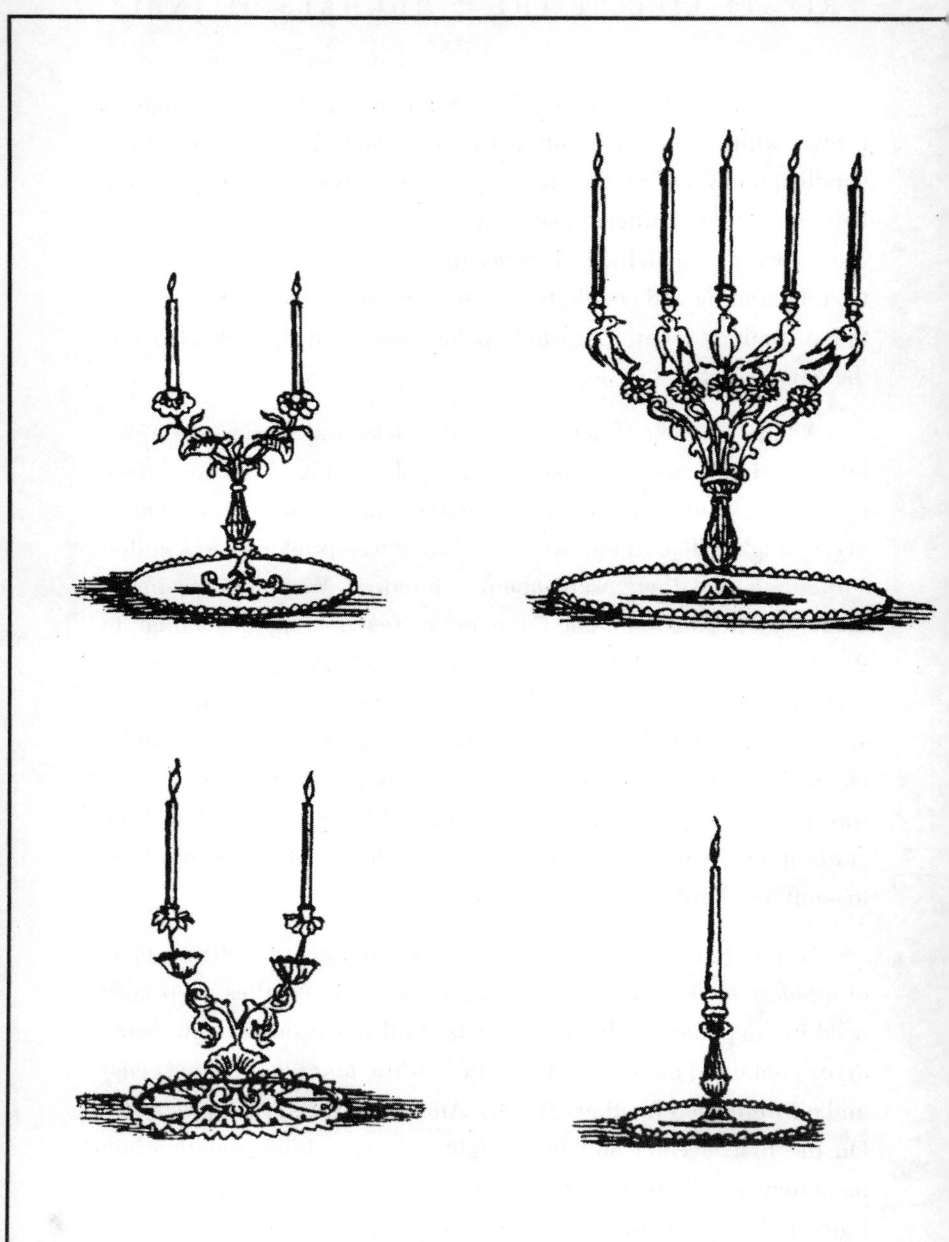

Fig. 7. Mughal Candle-sticks

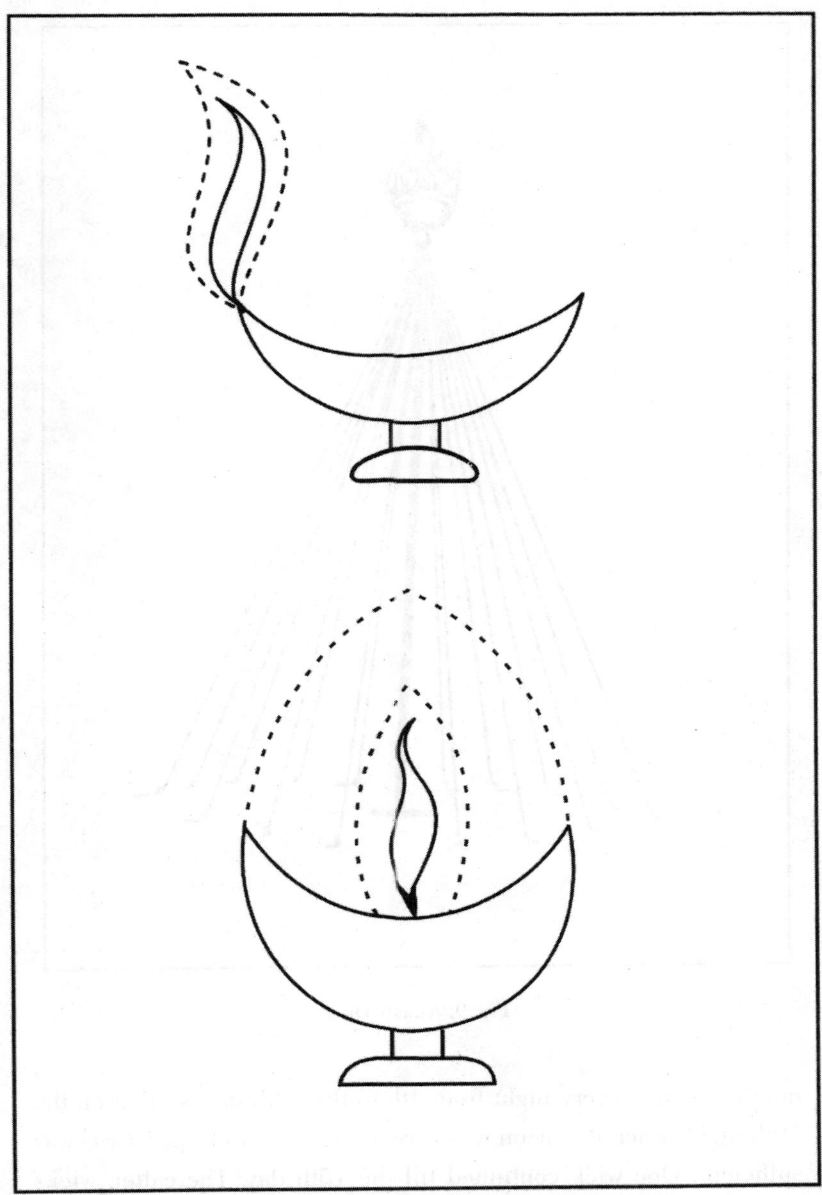

Fig. 8. Diyas

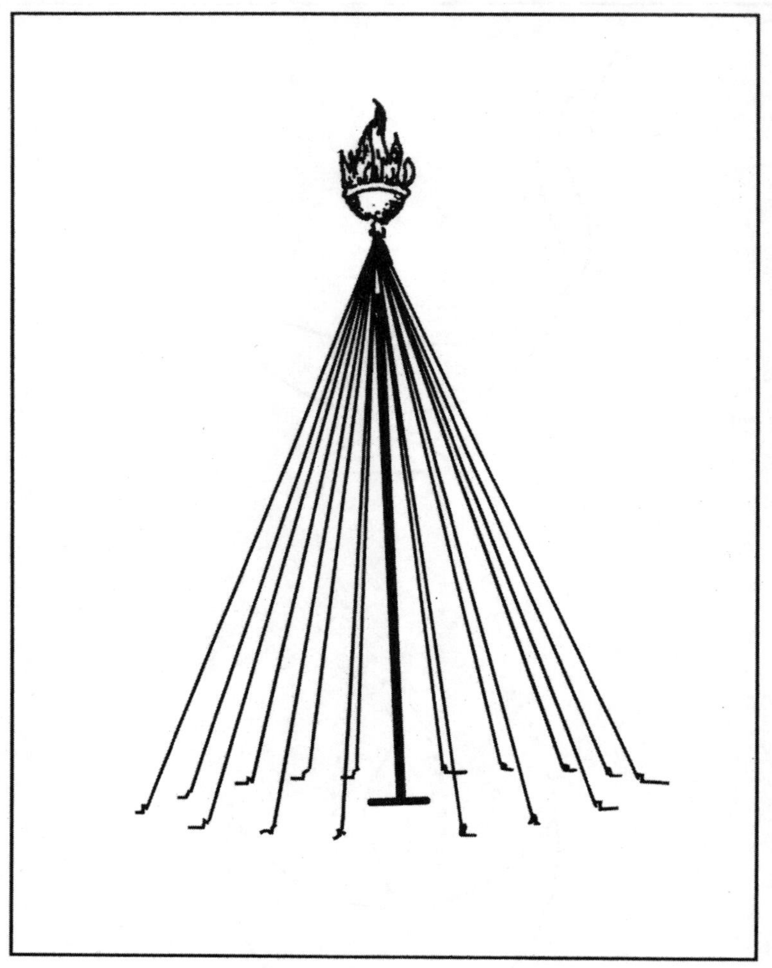

Fig. 9. Akash-Diya

number by one every night from 4th to the 10th day, so that on the 10th night, when the moon was very bright, one wick (per *diya*) was sufficient. One wick continued till the 15th day. Thereafter, wicks increased in number by one every night from 16th to the 19th. On the 20th night, the number of wicks was the same as on the 19th. On

21st and 22nd, they increased one daily. Number of wicks on 23rd was the same as on 22nd. From 24th to the last day of the month, 8 wicks were lighted up. These were gigantic *diyas* of metal (copper, brass or bronze), sometimes fitted on handsome stands, containing one *ser* of oil and half a *ser* of cotton for every wick, so that 8 *sers* of oil and 4 *sers* of cotton was used for a *diya* of 8 wicks. The number of *diyas* for each apartment was fixed and allowances were made accordingly. A set of experienced maid servants was constantly engaged in 'lighting' alone, and this was also a separate department called the *chiragh-khana* supervised by a *darogha* (officer incharge). The *harem* quarters in the Mughal camp were similarly lighted and the whole paraphernalia of palace illumination travelled with it.

Curtains and loose dresses (e.g. flowing *dupattas*) of the ladies sometimes caught fire and accidents occurred in the *harem* and these have been recorded. But no large scale fire in the palace owing to this medieval system of lighting has been reported, mainly owing to the care and caution of the attendants who were specifically trained and employed to look after only this aspect of the *harem* life.

In order to render the Mughal camp conspicuous to those who came from afar, a gigantic pole of 40 yards height was erected in front of the *durbar*, a little behind which were situated the *harem* quarters, in gorgeous tents. It was supported by sixteen ropes. On its top was placed a huge *diya*, with several *mans* of *binaula* (cotton-seed) and oil (Fig 9). It was called *Akash-Diya* (The Light of the Sky). It was lighted after sunset. It illuminated the whole camp.

12
Imperial Paraphernalia

It is simply not possible to describe the vast paraphernalia associated with the life of the Great Mughals in a single instance. A wide variety of floor furnishings, furniture, curtains, costumes and jewellery was used by them. Surprisingly, a *karkhanah* (workshop) for the production, or *kargah* (department) for the management, of each of these articles was separately established by Akbar.

(a) Floor Coverings, etc.

Akbar's historian recorded that the king caused carpets to be made of wonderful varieties and charming textures. He appointed experienced workmen (*karigar*) who produced masterpieces, which excelled the *gilims* of Iran and Turan. Though import of carpets from such Iranian centres as Goshkan, Khuzistan, Kirman and Sabzwar continued, Imperial *karkhanahs* were established for the production of carpets in all important towns of the Empire, particularly in Agra, Fatehpur Sikri and Lahore, where all kinds of carpet weavers had settled. This led to a flourishing trade of carpets. In the imperial workshops single *gilims* were made of 20 *gaz 7 tassujes* long, and 6 *gaz* 11½ *tassujes** broad at a cost of rupees 1810/- which were worth rupees 2715/- in the market. Similarly, various kinds of cotton *jajams, shatranjis* (*durries*) and *baluchis* were produced. Fine mats of cotton which looked like silk were also manufactured in the Imperial *karkhanahs. Takya-namads,* or woollen coverlets were brought from Kabul and Persia, but these were also made in India. A separate department of mattresses called the *toshak-khanah* was maintained. The credit of establishing these handicrafts, which are among the most profitable industries today, goes to the genius of Akbar.

It must be noted that rooms and halls of the palace were all gorgeously furnished. Country mattresses (*chatais*) were first spread on these floors, over which cotton *durries* (shatranjis) or *jajams* were used. Beautiful carpets of silk or wool, in accordance with the season, were spread over them. No internal floor was ever left bare. Doors and windows were furnished with silk or velvet curtains. The Mughal palaces, without these furnishings, today look barren and desolate.

* There were 24 *girih* (*girah*) or 24 *tassuj* in one *ilahi gaz* (yard) which was equal to 32 inches or 81.28 cms.

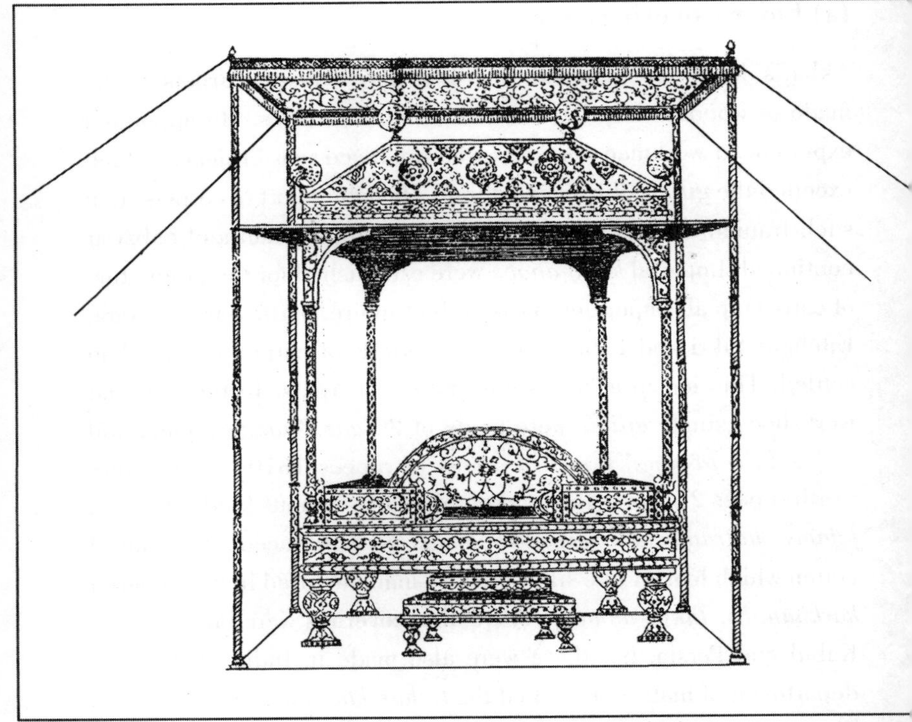

Fig. 10. Mughal Throne (Aurang)

It is noteworthy that, in the interior, an open court and series of *dalans* opening on it were indispensable characteristics of the king's, noble's and a richman's household. Sometimes, there were two and three rows of pillars in these *dalans*. Warmth and privacy was secured by means of thick wadded curtains, called *pardahs*, made to fit each arched opening between the pillars. These *pardahs* were sometimes made of woollen cloth, sometimes of coarse calico, in patch-work style, striped, vandyked or in some other ingeniously contrived and ornamented way, according to the taste. Besides these *pardahs*, the openings between the pillars had blinds neatly made of fine bamboo strips, woven together with coloured cords. These were

Fig. 11. Mughal Throne (Aurang)

called *chiks*. These were painted in various colours and in a variety of patterns. These blinds constituted a real comfort to everyone in the tropical climate of India as they admitted air when let down and at the same time shut out flies and other annoying insects. Besides, the extreme glare was also shaded by them. *Khas-Tatiyas* (screens of *Khas*) were also used on windows and external doors during summers, and sprinkled with water intermittently. This rendered the air cool and perfumed. The household was thus equipped in a number of ways to make living comfortable.

Quilts (*razais*) were used in winters. These were of the highest orders, generally made of silk of the brightest hues, well wadded, and lined with dyed muslin of assimilating colour. These were usually bound with broad silver ribands, and sometimes bordered with gold brocaded trimmings. Quilts were also made of fine chintz and, for servants and slaves, of coarse cloth, but all were of the same plan. Woollen shawls of Kashmir were used when the weather was mildly cold. Otherwise quilts were preferred. Blankets were not used in the palace. Blankets of black colour were used only by the poorest peasantry.

The Mughals used very little furniture and there were no chairs or tables. But thrones, *chowkis, diwans* and bedsteads were invariably used. These were made of such costly wood as sandal and ebony and tastefully designed, carved and inlaid. Thrones (*aurangs*) for the use of the king were specifically made of several beautiful forms (Fig. 10 & 11). Some were inlaid with precious stones. Others were made of gold and silver. *Chhatra* (royal umbrella), pillows (*masnads*) and foot-stools (*sandali*) were used with them. Jalied wooden curtains and decorated *sarapardas* (portable curtains made of coarse cloths or velvet and bamboo poles) were also in usage.

(b) *Farrash-Khanah*

There was a separate department called *farrash-khanah* for the maintenance of tents, furniture, carpets and such other stores. Its paraphernalia was used on journeys in the Mughal camp which was, in fact, a small replica or miniature of the imperial capital,

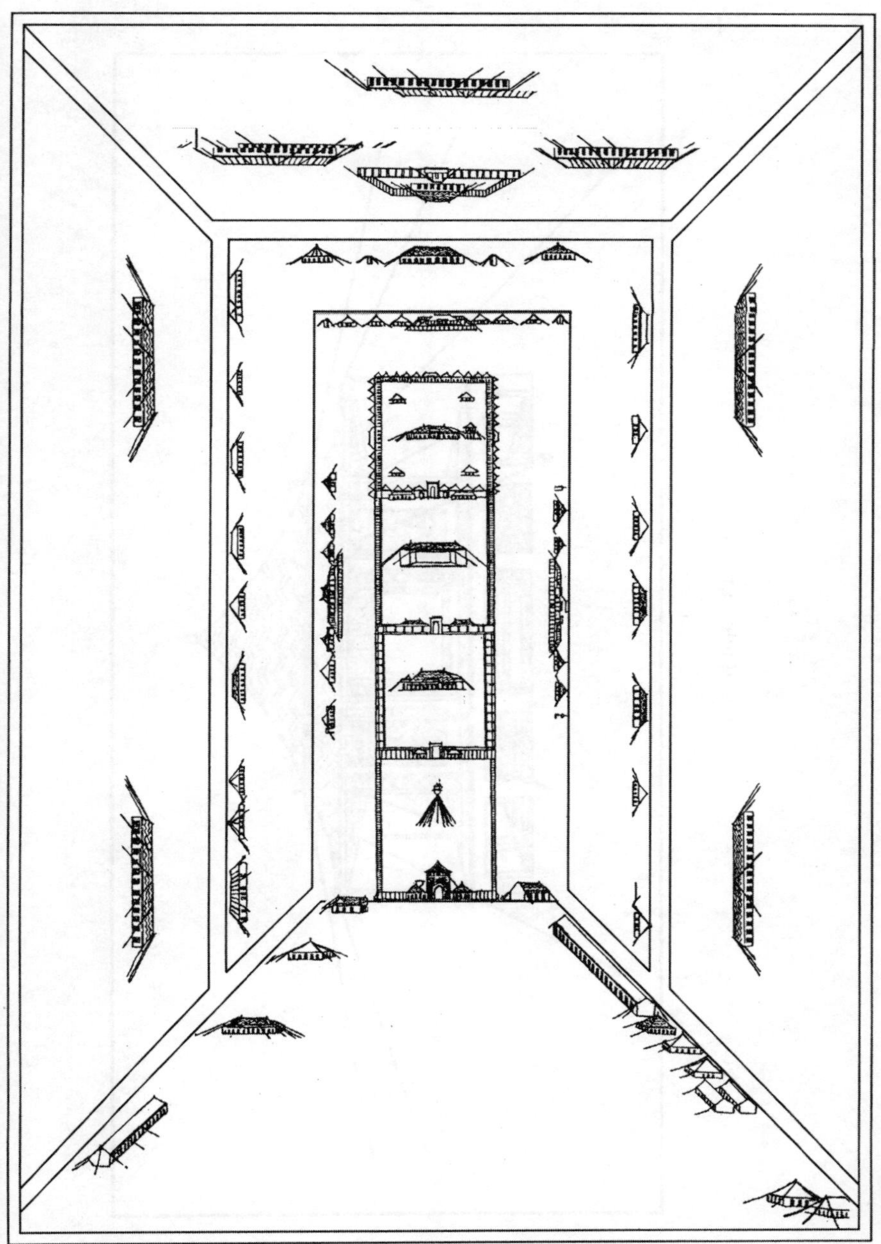

Fig. 12. Plan of the Mughal Camp

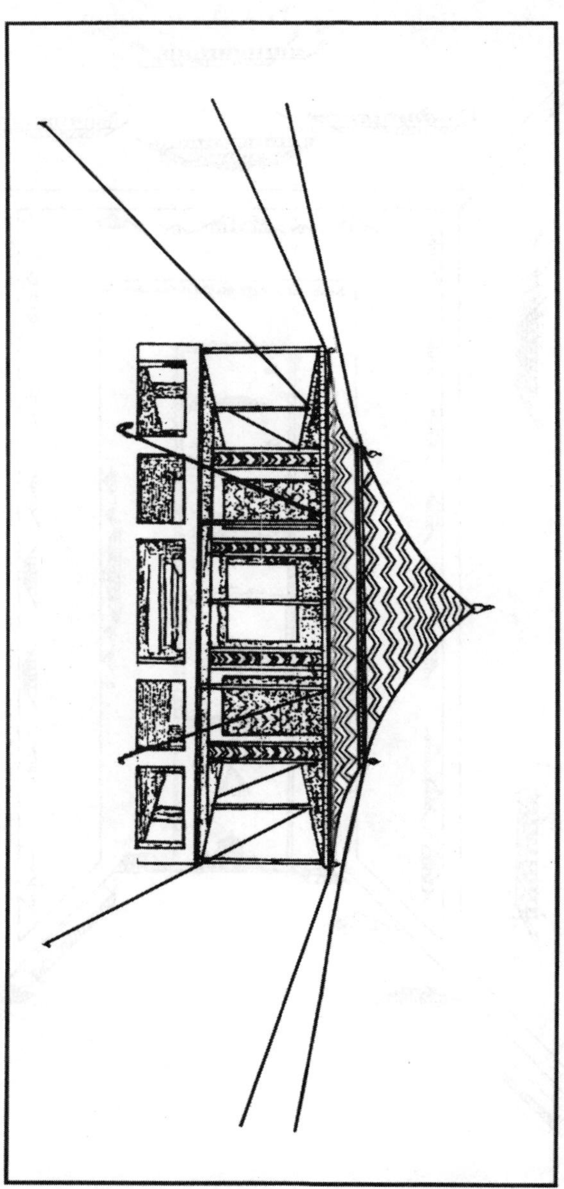

Fig. 13. Chubin Raoti

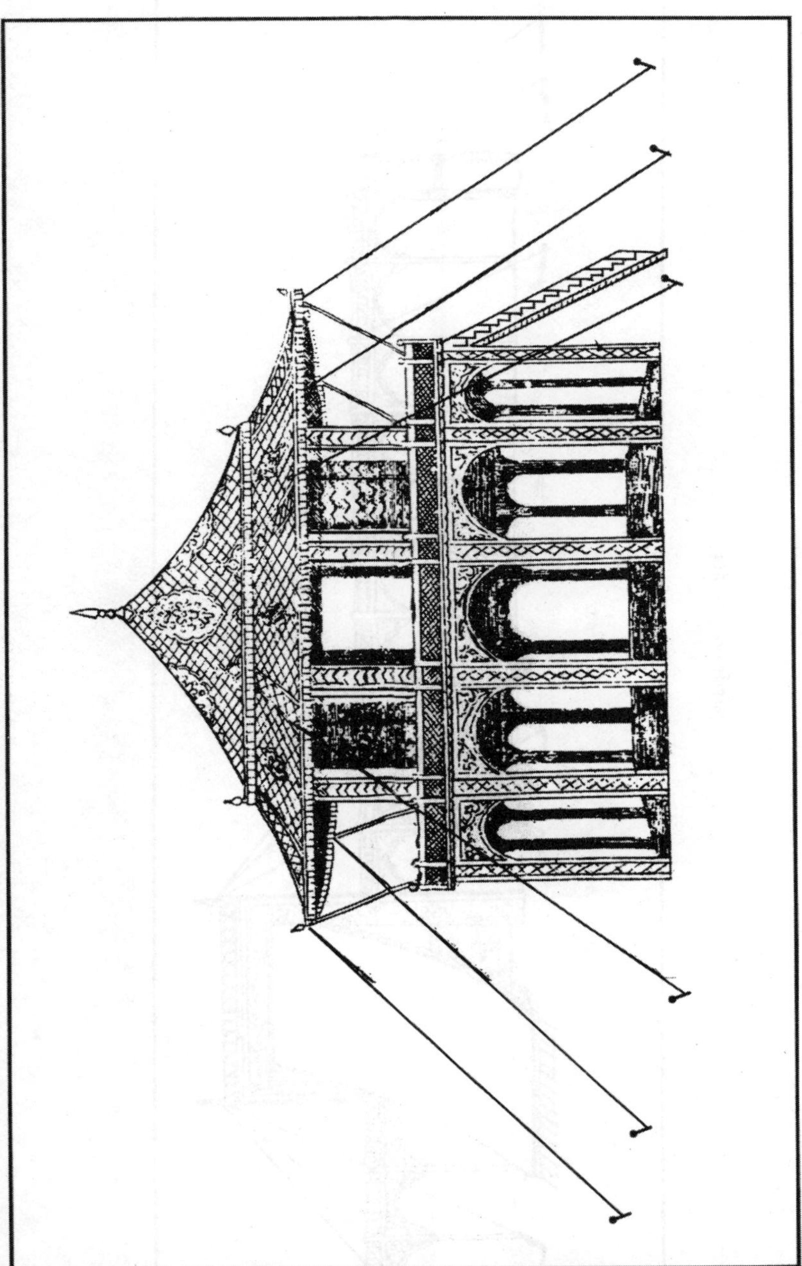

Fig. 14. Do-Ashiyana Manzil

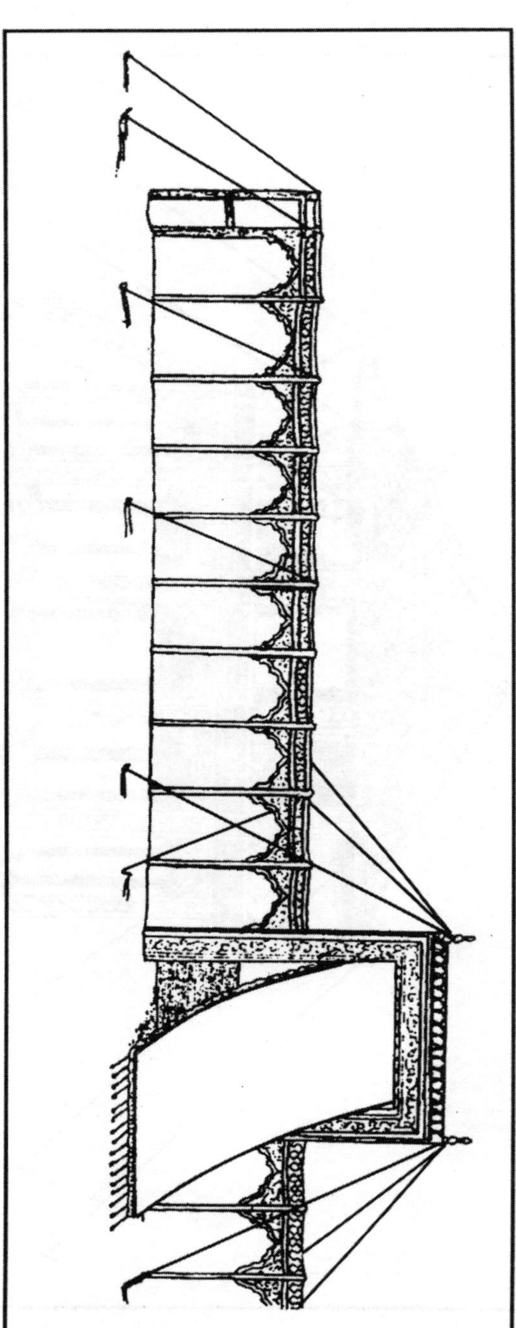

Fig. 15. Saraparda

including the palace (Fig. 12). A brief description of its composition and constituents will give an idea of its size and quality.

Bargah was a large tent which could accommodate 10,000 people. It took a thousand *farrashes* (workmen of the department) a week to erect it with the help of machines. A plain *bargah* without brocade, velvet and gold ornaments costed rupees 10,000; others were costlier.

Chubin Raoti was a wooden pavilion (Fig. 13) raised on 10 wooden pillars, two of which were of larger height as the crossbeams rested upon them. The pillars had, above and below, a *dasa* (a support; a triangular piece of wood fixed into the angle formed by the vertical beam and cross-beams) to keep in position. Several rafters passed over the *dasas* and the crossbeam, the whole being kept tightly together by clamps, nuts and bolts. The walls and the roof consisted of mats. There was one door or two, and at the height of the lower *dasas* there was a raised platform, made of wooden planks. The inside was ornamented with brocade and velvet and the outside with scarlet sackcloth, tied to the walls with silk tape.

Even a portable wooden house of two storeys called *Do-Ashiyana-Manzil* was in usage (Fig. 14). It was raised upon 18 pillars, six yards in height, which supported a wooden platform and into this, pillars of four cubits in length were fixed with nuts and bolts forming an upper storey. It was used by the king as sleeping apartment in camp, and also as place of worship, and for *Jharokha-darshan*. There were several types of tents of different dimensions. *Saraparda* (portable curtain) was made in former times of coarse canvas, but since Akbar's age, it was made of carpeting (Fig. 15). The *gulabar* was a wooden screen. Its parts were fastened together with leather straps. It was covered with red cloth, tied with tape.

The *Gulal-Bar* was a grand enclosure used in Mughal

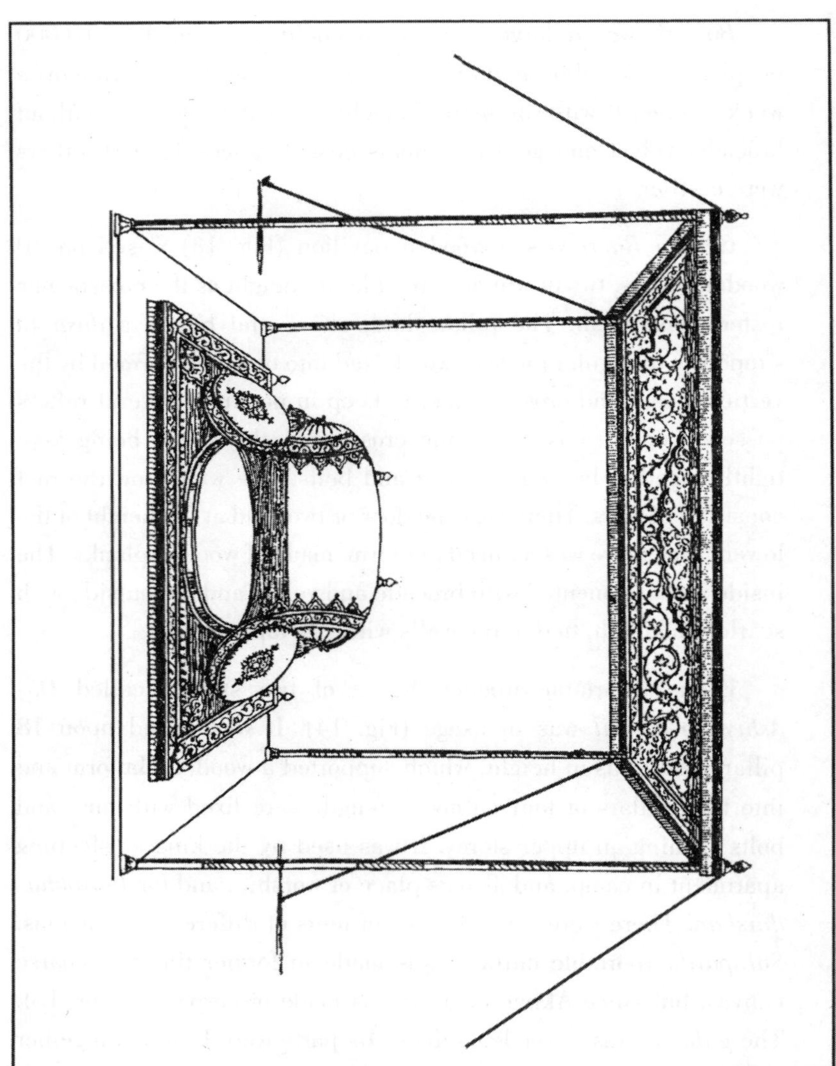

Fig. 16. Namgira

encampment. It was never less than 100 yards square. At its eastern end a pavilion of two entrances was erected containing 54 divisions, 24 yards long and 14 broad. A large *chubin-raoti* stood in its middle and a *saraparda* around it. The *do-ashiyana-manzil* where the king worshipped and performed *jharokha* was built up adjoining to this *chubin-raoti*. No one connected with the *harem* entered this building without special leave. Outside of it 24 *chubin-raotis* were erected 10 yards long and six yards wide, each separated by a canvas where the favourite women of the *harem* resided (while in the camp). There were other pavilions and tents with awnings (*sayabans*) of gold embroidery, brocade and velvet.

Adjacent to this, an area 60 yards square was enclosed by *saraparda*. Tents were erected in it for the *Urdu-Begis* (armed women) and other female servants. Further on upto the private audience hall there was a fine open space 150 x 100 yards called *mahtabi*. Screens were set up on its both sides, by poles six yards long fixed in the ground at an interval of two yards. Poles were one yard in the ground and were ornamented with brass-knobs on the top and kept firm by two ropes, one passing inside and the other outside the enclosure. Guards were posted here.

In the midst of the plain, was a raised platform which was protected by an awning called *namgira* supported by four poles (Fig.16). Here the king used to sit in the evening, and none but those who were particularly favoured were admitted. Adjoining to the *gulal-bar*, there was a circular enclosure consisting of 12 divisions, each of 30 yards. Its door opened into the *mahtabi*. In its middle was a *chubin-raoti*, 10 yards long, and a tent containing 40 divisions over which 12 awnings were spread each of 12 yards. These were separated by *qanats* (which were also upright, portable curtains like *sarapardas*). Adjacent to this, a *saraparda* was put up, 150 x 150 yards, containing 16 divisions of 36 square yards, it being sustained

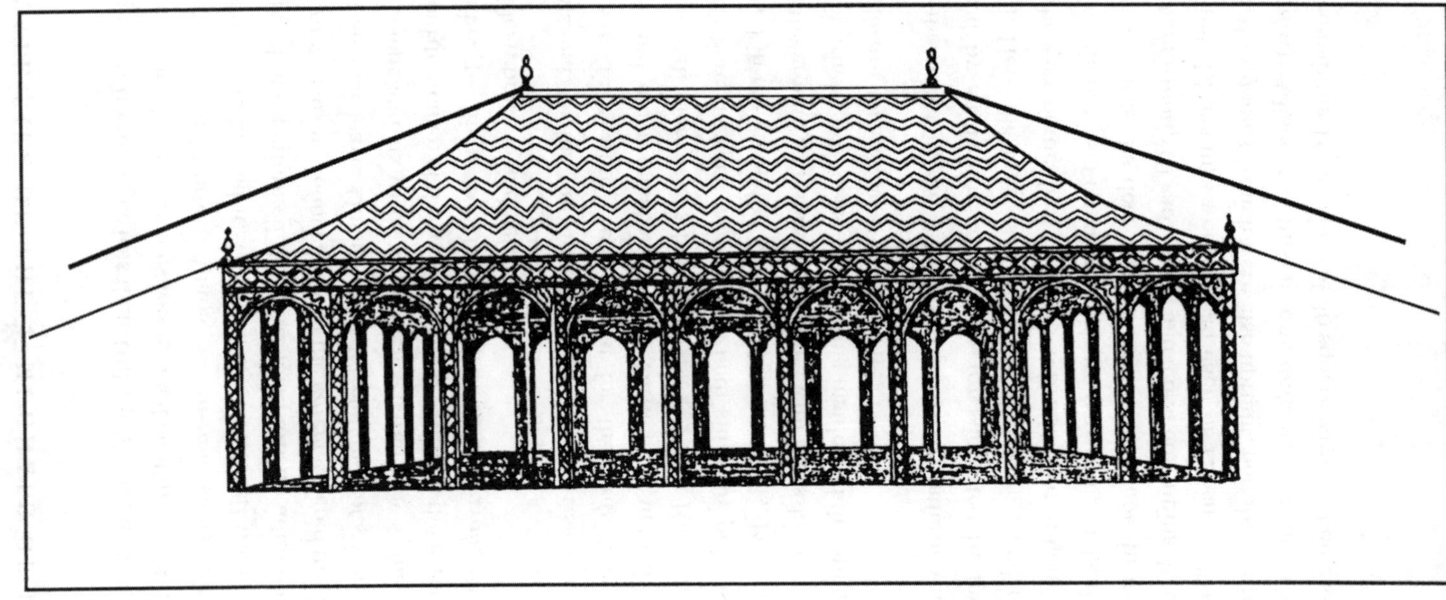

Fig. 17. Diwan-i-Khass

by poles and knobs. *Qanats* and *sarapardas* were lined with chintz worked over with flowers of a hundred different kinds, and others with figured satin, decorated with deep silken fringes.

In the midst of it, the state-hall was erected by means of a thousand carpets. It contained 72 rooms and had an opening 15 yards wide. A tent-like covering, or *Qalandari*, made of wax-cloth (*mom-jama*), or any other lighter material, was spread over it, to afford protection against the rain and the sun. Round about it were 50 awnings of 12 yards each. The *Diwan-i-Khass* (Fig.17) was decorated with carpets of various colours so that, as the historian noted, it resembled a beautiful flower-bed. Guards were stationed at fixed places for security. An idea of the vastness of this Mughal paraphernalia can be had from the fact that it required for its carriage 100 elephants, 500 camels, 400 carts and 100 bearers. It was escorted by 500 troopers. There were employed in this department, a thousand *farrashes*, natives of Iran, Turan and Hindustan, 500 pioneers (*bel-dars* or labourers), 100 water-carriers (*abkash* or *bhishtis*), 50 carpenters, tent-makers and torch-bearers, 30 workers in leather, and 150 sweepers, whose monthly pay varied from 240 to 130 *dams*.

(c) Wardrobe *(Kurkyaraq* or *Karkaraq-Khanah)*

It was again Akbar who, as on everything else, paid much attention to the establishment and working of this department. Though Iranian, European and Mongolian articles of wear were imported, efforts were made to produce various stuffs indigenously. Skilful masters and workmen were invited and patronised to settle in this country to teach people an improved system of manufacture. Imperial workshops (*karkhanas*) were established in the towns of Lahore, Agra, Fatehpur Sikri and Ahmedabad. They turned out masterpieces of workmanship. Their figures, patterns, knots and variety of fashions astonished experienced travellers, so recorded the contemporary historian. The workmanship of the stuffs improved tremendously under royal patronage. All kinds of hair-weaving and silk-spinning were brought to perfection and the imperial workshops furnished all those stuffs which were made in other countries and hitherto imported. A taste for fine material has since become general and the drapery used at feasts surpassed every description.

The Mughal wardrobe was as efficiently maintained as other departments. All articles which were brought, or were ordered to be woven, or received as tribute or presents were carefully preserved and recorded. They were periodically inspected. Lengths (*thans*) were given out to be cut and made up into costumes, which were given away as presents. Articles were arranged according to their prices. Experienced people continually inquired into the prices of articles used both formerly and at present, as a knowledge of the exact prices was conducive to the increase of the stock. Even the prices became generally lower. Thus a piece woven by the famous Ghiyath-i-Naqshband obtained for 50 gold *muhrs*, whilst it had formerly been sold for twice that amount. Most other goods got cheaper by 66-2/3 and even 75 percent. The King also ordered that people of certain ranks should wear certain articles. This was done in order to regulate the demand. Everybody was not allowed to wear everything and dress was more a public than a private matter. This was also done to denote ranks, castes and professions, and to keep the people within their social-limit (called *auqat*).

Akbar's historian has described a few articles of the king's dress as follows:

1. The *takauchiya* was a coat without lining, of the Indian form. Formerly, it had slits in the skirt and was tied on the left side. Akbar ordered it to be made with a round skirt and to be tied on the right side. It required 7 *gaz* (yards) and seven *girah,* and five *girah* for the binding. The price for making a plain one varied from 1 to 3 rupees.

But if the coat was adorned with ornamental stitching, from 1 to 4¾ rupees. Besides, a *misqal* of silk was required.

2. The *peshwaz* was also a coat of the same form open in front. It was tied in front. It was sometimes made without strings.

3. The *dutahi* was a coat with lining. It required 6 *gaz* and 4 *girah* for the outside, 6 *gaz* lining, 4 *girah* for binding, and 9 *girah* for the border. The price of making one varied from 1 to 3 rupees. One *misqal* of silk was required.

4. The *shah-ajida* (royal stitch coat) was also called *shast-khatt* (or 60 rows), as it had 60 ornamental stitches per *girah*. Generally, it had a double lining, and was sometimes wadded and quilted. The cost of making was 2 rupees per *gaz*.

5. The *Suzani* required a quarter of a *ser* of cotton and 2 *dams* of silk. It was also a coat with embroidery depicting leaves and flowers. If sewed with *bakhiya* stitches (back-stitching), the price of making one was 8 rupees. One with *ajida* (buttonhole stitches) costed 4 rupees.

6. The *qalami* required 3/8 *ser* cotton and 1 *dam* silk. The cost of its making was 2 rupees.

7. The *qaba* which was generally called *Jama-i-pumbadar* was a wadded coat. It required 1 *ser* of cotton and 2 *misqals* of silk. Cost of its making was 1 to 1¼ rupee.

8. The *gadar* was a coat wider and longer than the *qaba* and contained more wadding. In Hindustan, it took the place of a fur-coat. It required 7 *gaz* of stuff, 6 *gaz* of lining, 4 *girah* for binding, 9 for bordering, 2½ *ser* of cotton and 3 *misqals* of silk. Cost of its sewing was ½ to 1½ rupees.

9. The *farji* had no binding and was open in front. Some put buttons to it. It was worn over the *jama* (coat) and required 5 *gaz* 12

girah stuff; 5 *gaz* 5 *girah* lining; 14 *girah* bordering; 1 *ser* cotton and 1 *misqal* silk. Cost of its making was ¼ to 1 rupee.

10. The *fargul* resembled the *yapanji* (a rain-coat) but it was more comfortable and becoming. It was brought from Europe but soon it became so popular that everyone used to wear it. It was made of several stuffs. It required 9 *gaz* 6½ *girah* stuff, the same quantity of lining, 6 *misqals* of silk and 1 *ser* of cotton. It was made both single and double. Cost of its sewing was from ½ to 2 rupees.

11. The *chakman* was made of broadcloth or woollen stuff or wax cloth. Akbar ordered it to be made of *dara'i* wax cloth which was very light and pretty. Rain water could not get through it. It required 6 *gaz* stuff, 5 *girah* binding and 2 *misqal* of silk. The cost of making one of broadcloth was 2 rupees; of wool 1½ rupees; of wax cloth ½ rupee. Out of a large number and wide variety of coats, waist-coats, jackets (*phatuhi*) and tunics (*angarakha*) used during the medieval period, only a few have remained in fashion these days, and *chakman* is one of them in a simplified form, under the modern name of *achakan*.

12. The *shalwar* (drawers) was made of all kinds of stuff, single and double, and wadded. It required 3 *gaz* 11 *girah* cloth, 6 *girah* for the hem through which the string ran, 3 *gaz* 5 *girah* lining, 1¾ *misqal* silk and ½ *ser* cotton. Cost of its making was from ¼ to ½ rupee.

There were various kinds of each of these garments. Similarly a large number of *chiras, fawtas* and *dupattas* (stuffs of different shapes used for making turbans or *pagadis, safas* and *murethas*) was available. Costly dresses worn at feasts or presented to the nobles and servants of the state as a mark of honour were also of a wide variety. Every season, a thousand complete suits (*saropa,* dresses from head to foot) were made for the imperial wardrobe and 120, in 12 bundles of 10 each, were always kept in readiness. This gives an idea of the magnitude of the Mughal wardrobe.

Humayun and Akbar are recorded to have changed their dresses daily to match with the colour of the planet of the day. Otherwise too, washermen's services were limited to the middle classes and the imperial personnel and the nobles changed their apparel too often and loved to wear new clothes. Akbar also used the Hindu *dhoti* in the *harem* for its comfortable wear. It was of silk. The Mughal emperors, including Aurangzeb, believed in wearing gorgeous dresses, obviously, for impression.

Akbar liked the indigenous things the most. He was very fond of giving Sanskrit and *deshi* names to various things he introduced or reformed. He is recorded to have changed the names of several garments and invented, like his coins, new and pleasing terms for them, e.g.

Original Name	**(Akbar's version)**
Jama (coat)	- *Sarbgati* (covering the whole body)
Izar (drawers)	- *Yar-Pirahan* (Companion of the Coat)
Nimtana (jacket)	- *Tanzeb* (Pocket of the Body)
Fauta (loin-cloth)	- *Patgat*
Burqa (veil)	- *Chitragupta* (Secret Beauty or Picture)
Kulah (cap)	- *Shish Shobha* (Ornament of Head)
Muy-Baf (hair-ribbon)	- *Keshghan*
Patka (a cloth for the loins)	- *Katzeb* (Pocket of Waist)

Shal (Shawl)	- *Parmnarm* (extremely soft)
Kapardhur (a Tibetan stuff)	- *Kapurnur* (White Beauty)
Pay-Afzar (Shoes)	- *Charn-dharn*

These indigenous names were ingeniously coined and used in order to popularise the innovations of the Mughal age in the land of Hindustan.

The ladies of the *harem* used a great variety of dresses. Rajput ladies used sari, *lahanga* or *ghaghra* (petticoat), *angiya* (bodice) and *odni* or *phariya* (scarf). Muslim ladies also used *ghaghra* but they preferred *paijama* (trousers) or *shalwars* (breeches) and *qamiz* (shirt). Women's *paijama* did not much differ from that of men. It was tied at the navel by means of a silver or silken thread or cord (*nada*) running through it. *Shalwars* were more common. These were made of cotton, silk or brocade according to the taste and were striped in several colours. Shirts were made of chintz, linen (*malmal*), calico (*dares*), velvet (*makhmal*), damask (*jamdani*), diaper brocade (*kamdani*) and lappet (*chikan*) in different forms and fashions. They also put on *qabas* of fine Kashmir wool in winter. These were plaited on the waist and were of different types. Shawls of such rich varieties as *tus* were also in fashion. Nur Jehan is recorded to have paid great attention to ladies' wear and devised many kinds of fashionable dresses. Several varieties of brocades, laces and gowns owe their origin to her. The most famous were *Nur-Mahali, Her-Dudami, Panchtolia, Badlah, Kainari* and *Farsh-i-Chandni*. Muslim ladies used *dupattas* of fine cotton or silk, wrought with silver or gold threads. They also used *chadars* and *burqas* to cover their heads. Several types of head-dresses were in usage. Princesses and daughters of nobles used one called *lachaq*. It was a square mantle doubled into a triangle and fastened at the chin. Ladies used light shoes of various patterns and artistic slippers covered with silver and golden flowers. These were of red and gold colours and without backs. An effect of gorgeousness was again the watchword and the costliest material was used in the making of ladies' costumes.

(d) Shawls and stuffs

Many improvements were made in this department under Akbar's guidance. The imperial wardrobe began to patronise *tus* (or Shah Tus) shawls on a large scale. It was the costliest of the shawls made of the wool of a species of sheep of that name, found in the Himalayan region. Its natural colours were black, white and red, but chiefly black. Sometimes the colour was a pure white. This kind of shawl was unrivalled for its lightness, warmth and softness. It was so soft that a full shawl could pass through a finger-ring. People used to wear it without altering its natural colour. Akbar ordered it to be dyed but, curiously, it did not take a red dye. Improvements were made in the preparation of the *safid alchas* (or *alacha*) also called *tarhdars*, or the corded stuffs. The wool was either white or black and these stuffs could be had in three colours, white, black and mixed. The white kind was formerly dyed in three ways; under Akbar's order it was dyed in several other ways.

A large number of costly stuffs with gold and silk threads and brocades were prepared in the imperial *karkhanas*, the most popular among them were *zardozi* and *kalabattun* which were silk stuffs embroidered with *zari* (floral designs embroidered with gold and silver threads, stars, leaves and flowers); *kashida* and *qalghai* which were also *zari* (embroidered) stuffs with gold and silk threads; *bandhnun* (*bandhej*) which were stuffs dyed differently in different parts of the piece; *chhint* (*chintz*) which were printed stuffs; and *purzdar* which were stuffs the outside of which was plush-like. These innovations gave birth to an industry which spread, with the Mughals, far and wide in the country and is still sustaining the economy of a section of the Indian population.

The garments stored in the imperial wardrobe were arranged according to the days, months and years of their entries, and according to their colour, price and weight. This arrangement was called *misl* or a set. The clerks of the department prepared a label on a strip of cloth according to the degree of every article of wear and tagged it to the end of the pieces. Whatever pieces of the same kind of good quality arrived for the imperial wardrobe on the *Urmuzd* day (first day) of the month of *Farwardin*, had a higher rank assigned to them than those pieces which arrived on other days. If the pieces were equal in value, their precedence or otherwise was determined by the character of the day of their entry; if the pieces were equal as far as the character of the day was concerned, they put the lighter stuff higher in rank. If the pieces had the same weight, they arranged them according to their colour.

The following was the order of colours

Tus (Tusi)

Safed-Alcha (Safed, white)

Ruby coloured

Golden (*Sunahri*)

Orange (*Narangi*)

Brass coloured (*Pitliya*)

Crimson (dark red)

Grass-Green (sap green)

Cotton-flower coloured (mauve colour)

Sandalwood-coloured (*Chandani*, yellow ochre)

Almond-coloured (*Badami*, light brown)

Purple (*Bengani*)

Grape-coloured (*Anguri*, light green)

Mauve (a shade of purple)

Parrot-coloured (*Totai*, light green)

Honey-coloured (dark brown)

Brownish Lilac (dark brown)

Coloured like the *Ratanmanjani* Flower

Coloured like the *Kasni* Flower

Apple-coloured (light red)

Hay-coloured (chrome yellow)

Pistachio (*Pishtai*, dark green)

Bhojapatra-coloured (brown)

Pink (*Gulabi*)

Light Blue

Coloured like the *Galghah* flower

Water-coloured

Oil-coloured

Brown-red

Emerald-coloured

Bluish like China-ware (*Lajward* colour)

Violet (*Bengani*)

Bright Pink

Mango-coloured (chrome yellow deep)

Musk-coloured

Coloured like the *Fakhta* Bird (Ring-dove, grey)

This list contains, in fact, many pleasing shades of different colours which were in fashion during the medieval period. Obviously, light shades of yellow, brown, blue, green and red were preferred.

Shawls were brought from Kashmir. Every encouragement was given there by the Mughal state for their manufacture. These were also produced in large quantities in Lahore (Punjab) where there were more than a thousand workshops. A particular kind of shawl called *mayan* was chiefly woven there. It consisted of silk and wool. It was used for *chiras* (turbans) and *fotas* (loin-bands). People of the Mughal age used shawls customarily. Originally they folded them up in four folds and wore them for a very long time, but now they were generally worn without folds, and merely thrown over the shoulder. Akbar started the fashion of wearing them double, which looked very good.

The following is the list of gold, silk, cotton and woollen stuffs and their prices during Akbar's age (c. 1600 A.D.):

Gold Stuffs

Brocaded velvet from Yazd per piece (length, *than*)	- 15 to 150 gold *muhrs*
Brocaded velvet from Europe per piece	- 10 to 70 gold *muhrs*
Brocaded velvet from Gujarat per piece	- 10 to 50
Brocaded velvet from Kashan per piece	- 10 to 40
Brocaded velvet from Herat per piece	- price not known
Brocaded velvet from Lahore per piece	- 10 to 40 gold *muhrs*
Brocaded velvet from Barsah per piece	- 3 to 70
Mutabbaq brocade from Khallukh and Turkistan	- 2 to 70
Milak brocade per piece	- 3 to 70

Brocade from Gujarat per piece	- 4 to 60
Tas brocade from Gujarat per piece	- 1 to 35
Dara'i-baf (brocaded silk from Gujarat)	- 2 to 50
Muqayyash (silk with stripes of silver from Gujarat)	- 1 to 20
Sherwani brocade from Gujarat	- 6 to 17
Mushajjar (silk with leaves and branches woven in it) from Europe per *gaz*	- 1 to 4
Deba (coloured) silk from Europe per *gaz*	- 1 to 4
Deba silk from Yazd per *gaz*	- 1 to 1½
Khara per *gaz*	- 5 *rupiya* to 2 *muhrs*
Satin from Chinese Tartary	- price not known
Nawar from Chinese Tartary	- price not known
Khazz Silk	- price not known
Tafsila (a stuff from Mecca) per *gaz*	- 15 to 20 *rupiya*
Kurtahwar from Gujarat per piece	- 1 to 20 *muhr*
Mindil per piece	- 1 to 14 *muhr*
Chira (for turbans) per piece	- ½ to 8 *muhr*
Dupatta per piece	- 8 to 9 *rupiya*
Fotas (loin-bands) per piece	- ½ to 12 *muhr*
Counterpanes per piece	- 1 to 20 *muhr*

Silks

Velvet from Europe per *gaz* (yard)	- 1 to 4 *muhr*
Velvet from Kashan per piece (*than*)	- 2 to 7 *muhr*
Velvet from Yazd per piece	- 2 to 4

Velvet from Mashhad per piece	- 2 to 4 *muhr*
Velvet from Herat per piece	- 1½ to 3
Velvet from Khafi per piece	- 2 to 4
Velvet from Lahore per piece	- 2 to 4
Velvet from Gujarat per *gaz*	- 1 to 2 *rupiya*
Qatifayi-i-Purabi per *gaz*	- 1 to 1½
Taja-baf per piece	- 2 to 30 *muhr*
Dara'i-baf per piece	- 2 to 30
Mutabbaq per piece	- 1 to 30
Sherwani per piece	- 1½ to 10
Milak per piece	- 1 to 7
Kamkhab from Kabul and Persia per piece	- 1 to 5
Tawar per piece	- 2 *rupiya* to 2 *muhr*
Khuri per piece	- 4 to 10 *rupiya*
Mushajjar from Europe per *gaz*	- 2 *rupiya* to 1 *muhr*
Mushajjar from Yazd per piece	- 1 to 2 *muhr*
Satin from Europe per *gaz*	- 2 *rupiya* to 1 *muhr*
Satin from Herat per piece	- 5 *rupiya* to 2 *muhr*
Khara per *gaz*	- 1 to 6 *rupiya*
Sihrang (changing silk, *Jhilmil*) per piece	- 1 to 3 *muhr*
Qutni per piece	- 1½ *rupiya* to 2 *muhr*
Katan (fine muslin) from Europe per *gaz*	- ½ to 1 *rupiya*
Tafta (taffeta) per *gaz*	- ¼ to 2 *rupiya*
Anbari per *gaz*	- 4 *dam* to ½ *rupiya*

Dara'i per *gaz*	- 8 *dam* to 2 *rupiya*
Sitipuri per piece	- 6 *rupiya* to 2 *muhr*
Qababand per piece	- 6 *rupiya* to 2 *muhr*
Tat Bandpuri per piece	- 2 *rupiya* to 1½ *muhr*
Lah per *gaz*	- 1/3 to 1/7 *rupiya*
Misri per piece	- ½ to 1 *muhr*
Sar per *gaz*	- 4 to 8 *dam*
Tassar per piece	- 1/3 to 2 *rupiya*
Plain *Kurtawar* satin per *gaz*	- ½ to 1 *rupiya*
Kapurnur (Kapurdhur) per *gaz*	- 5 *dam* to 1 *rupiya*
Alcha per *gaz*	- 8 *dam* to 2 *rupiya*
Tafsila per piece	- 7 to 12 *rupiya*
Cotton Clothes	
Khasa per piece (*than*)	- 3 *rupiya* to 15 *muhr*
Chautar per piece	- 2 *rupiya* to 9 *muhr*
Malmal per piece	- 4 *rupiya*
Tansukh per piece	- 4 *rupiya* to 5 *muhr*
Siri Saf per piece	- 2 *rupiya* to 5 *muhr*
Gangajal per piece	- 4 *rupiya* to 5 *muhr*
Bhiraun per piece	- 4 *rupiya* to 4 *muhr*
Sahan per piece	- 1 to 3 *muhr*
Jhona per piece	- 1 *rupiya* to 1 *muhr*
Atan per piece	- 2½ *rupiya* to 1 *muhr*
Asawali per piece	- 1 to 5 *muhr*
Bafta per piece	- 1½ *rupiya* to 5 *muhr*

Muhmudi per piece	- ½ to 3 *muhr*
Panchtoliya per piece	- 1 to 3 *muhr*
Jhola per piece	- ½ to 2½ *muhr*
Salu per piece	- 3 *rupiya* to 2 *muhr*
Doriya per piece	- 6 *rupiya* to 2 *muhr*
Bahadur Shahi per piece	- 6 *rupiya* to 2 *muhr*
Garba Suti per piece	- 1½ to 2 *muhr*
Shela from the Dakhin per piece	- ½ to 2 *muhr*
Mihirkul per piece	- 3 *rupiya* to 2 *muhr*
Mindil per piece	- ½ to 2 *muhr*
Sarband per piece	- ½ to 2 *muhr*
Dupatta per piece	- 1 *rupiya* to 1 *muhr*
Katancha per piece	- 1 *rupiya* to 1 *muhr*
Fota per piece	- ½ to 6 *rupiya*
Goshpech	- 1 to 2 *rupiya*
Chhint per *gaz*	- 2 *dam* to 1 *rupiya*
Gazina per piece	- ½ to 1½ *rupiya*
Silahati per *gaz*	- 2 to 4 *dam*
Woollen Stuffs	
Scarlet broadcloth from Turkey, Europe and Portugal, per *gaz*	- 2¼ *rupiya* to 4 *muhr*
Scarlet broadcloth from Nagaur and Lahore, per piece (*than*)	- 2 *rupiya* to 1 *muhr*
Suf-i-Murabba' per piece	- 4 to 15 *muhr*
Parmnarm per piece	- 2 *rupiya* to 20 *muhr*
Chira-yi-Parmnarm per piece	- 2 *rupiya* to 25 *muhr*

Fota per piece	- ½ to 3 *muhr*
Jamawar-i-Parmnarm per piece	- ½ to 4 *muhr*
Goshpech per piece	- 1½ *rupiya* to 1½ *muhr*
Sarpech per piece	- ½ to 4 *muhr*
Aghri per piece	- 7 *rupiya* to 2½ *muhr*
Parmgarm per piece	- 3 *rupiya* to 2½ *muhr*
Katas per piece	- 2½ *rupiya* to 10 *muhr*
Phuk per piece	- 2½ to 15 *rupiya*
Durman per piece	- 2 *rupiya* to 4 *muhr*
Patu per piece	- 1 to 10 *rupiya*
Rewkar per piece	- 2 *rupiya* to 1 *muhr*
Misri per piece	- 5 to 50 *rupiya*
Burd-i-Yamani per piece	- 5 to 35 *rupiya*
Manji Namad per piece	- 2 *rupiya* to 1 *muhr*
Kanpak Namad per piece	- 2 *rupiya* to 1 *muhr*
Takya Namad from Kabul and Persia	- price not known
Country made *Takya Namad* per piece	- 1½ to 5 *rupiya*
Lo'i per piece	- 14 *dam* to 4 *rupiya*
Blanket per piece	- 10 *dam* to 2 *rupiya*
Kashmiri caps per piece	- 2 *dam* to 1 *rupiya*

(e) Precious Stones and Jewellery

A word must be said on the precious stones (*ratnas*) used by the Mughals in their day to day life. Both their quantity and value were incredible. A separate department *Jawahar-Khanah* was efficiently maintained with an intelligent, trustworthy and clever treasurer; and an experienced clerk, a *darogha* and several skilful jewellers (*johri*) as his assistants. So vast was the collection of precious stones that they were classified into twelve classes according to their value. For example, rubies (*manik* or *chunni; yaqut*) were classified as follow:

1st class	–	not less than 1000 gold *muhrs* in value (for the piece)
2nd class	–	999-500 *muhrs*
3rd class	–	499-300
4th class	–	299-200
5th class	–	199-100
6th class	–	99-60
7th class	–	59-40
8th class	–	39-30
9th class	–	29¾-15
10th class	–	9¾-5
11th class	–	4¾-1
12th class	–	¾ *muhr*-¼ *rupiya*

In fact, rubies were the costliest stones during the Mughal period and they were also more popularly used than diamonds (*hira; almas*) or emeralds (*panna; zamurrad*). That the rubies of the first class were priced at 1000 gold *muhrs,* equivalent to 1000 *tolas* of gold and Rs. 5,000,000 (rupees fifty *lakhs*) at the modern rate of gold, is simply fabulous. There is no exaggeration and a large number of references in contemporary histories, memoirs and travel accounts confirm these prices. Rubies, diamonds and emeralds of the value of rupees one lakh to fifty thousand were most commonly stored in the *Jawahar-Khanah.*

A separate table for diamonds (*hira*), emeralds (*panna*) and red and blue rubies (*yaqut, manik*) was maintained in the *Jawahar-Khanah* for stones of lesser value, ranging from 30 gold *muhrs* to ¼ *rupiya.* Pearls (*moti*) were divided into 16 classes and strung by scores (twenties). The 1st class string contained 20 pearls each of the value of 30 *muhrs* and upwards; 2nd class varied from 29¾ to 15 *muhrs;* 3rd class from 14¾ to 12; 4th class, from 11¾ to 10; 5th class from 9¾ to 7; 6th class from 6¾ to 5; 7th class from 4¾ to 3; 8th class from 2¾ to 2; 9th class from 1¾ to 1; 10th class less than a *muhr* down to 5 *rupiya;* 11th class less than 5 to 2 *rupiya;* 12th class, less than 2 *rupiya* to 1¾ *rupiya;* 13th class less than 1¼ *rupiya* to 30 *dams;* 14th class less than 30 *dams* to 20 *dams;* 15th class less than 20 *dams* to 10 *dams;* and 16th class less than 10 *dams* to 5 *dams.* The pearls were strung upon a number of strings indicating their class, so that those of the 16th class were strung upon 16 strings. At the end of each bundle of strings the imperial seal was affixed, to avoid losses arising from unsorting, whilst a description was attached to prevent disorder.

William Hawkins who stayed in the court of Jehangir for a considerable period of time recorded that the King possessed 1½ *mans** (=37.8 kilograms) of diamonds, rough and cut, large and small but none less than 2½ carats; 12 *mans* (= 302.4 kgs) of pearls; 2 *mans* (50.4 kgs) of rubies; 5 *mans* (126 kgs) of emeralds and numerous other precious stones. Semi-precious stones like *abri, ajuba, amethyst, aqiq* (*yemeni,* agate), *bairuz* (aquamarine),

* He gave these figures in the *battman* weight, which was equivalent to Indian *man* (= 2160 tolas or 25.2 kilograms).

billaur (quartz), cornelian, *firoza* (turquoise), *jasper, lajward* (lapis lazuli) *maknatis, margaz,* opal, *pai-zahar, simaq, sulaimani* (onyx), *tamra* (garnet), *tilai* (goldstone), and *yashab* (jade) were not used for jewellery, but for making cups, wine-vases, bowls, trays, glasses and such other untensils which the Mughals commonly used in the household. These were incised or inlaid and set with jewels. Hawkins recorded that Jehangir who was most fond of such artistic curios had 200 glasses, 100 wine-vases and 500 drinking cups (of which 50 were made of one piece only) made of ballace ruby, emeralds, jade, turquoise and other stones. All this appears to be incredible today as if it is a piece picked up from some fable. Because, for more than a century, we are living under impoverished conditions, this is incomprehensible to us. Such was indeed the wealth the Mughals possessed and used in their daily life.

The Mughals and their ladies were also very fond of ornaments which they used to wear on their person from the head to the toe. Only the king and those whom he favoured and permitted used golden *kadas* (rings) on feet. Such *kadas* for wearing on wrists were presented by him to the nobles and servants of the state as a mark of honour and reward. The number and types of ladies' ornaments were legion. It must be noted, however, that gold was not as much favoured in male and female jewellery as were precious stones. Though golden ornaments which were either enamelled (with *minakari* called *kundan*) or inlaid with precious stones (*jadau*) were also popular, such jewellery of precious stones as strings, necklaces (*har*), garlands (*malas*), *kadas* and *kaundhanis* (made by *puvai*) were used on a large scale for the sheer charm of their glittering and twinkling effect in the dim lights of the medieval illuminations, and also for their fantastic value.

13
Daily Routine of the Mughal Emperors

Babur (1482-1530) and Humayun (1508-1555), the first two Great Mughals of India led a very turbulent life. They were constantly moving from one battlefield to the other and they could not settle down. It was Akbar (1542-1605) who founded the institutions which determined the course of the life of his descendants. As his historian has recorded, he used to get up before sunrise and devoted himself to meditation. This was a sort of prayer, though he was not particular to offer it ritualistically. Feeling ardently after God, and searching for truth, he exercised upon himself both inward and outward austerities. He joined the public worship, i.e. *namaz* only occasionally, 'in order to hush the slandering tongues of the bigots'. His devotion, thus, mostly consisted of self-examination, correction, and adoration of God. As the court historian recorded, he specially did so at the time when morning spread her azure silk and scattered abroad her, young, golden beams; and at noon when the light of the world-illuminating sun embraced the universe; and thus became a source of joy for all men; and in the evening when that fountain of light withdrew from the eyes of the mortal man to bewildering grief of all who were friends of light; and lastly, at midnight when that great cause of life turned again to ascend.

Meditation and veneration to the sun, fire and light was thus a form of religious worship which Akbar followed, four times a day. Musicians assembled about a watch before daybreak and played on songs and religious strains. Soon after the daybreak, the king appeared in the *jharokha* and accepted the obeisance of the people. Then he attended to various state matters, after which he retired to his private apartments and reposed a little.

Around noon, he went to the *Diwan-i-Khass* to attend important state business. Thereafter he retired to take his lunch and siesta. He spent the evening in looking after the working of various *karkhanas* (literally, workshops; various departments of the government engaged in production of arts and crafts) which he had instituted and in certain other cultural activities. After evening meditation and a little relaxation, he went to the Shah Burj where philosophers, *sufis* and *pundits* of different religions and learned men were admitted. They entertained the king with wise discourses. There were also present, in these assemblies, unprejudiced historians who did not mutilate history by adding or suppressing facts, and related the impressive events of ancient times. The king often made wonderfully shrewd remarks or started a fitting subject for conversation. On other occasions, matters related to the empire and revenue were brought up on which the king gave orders.

Then he retired to his private apartments. He drank a little. He was also fond of beautiful young women and spent some time in their company before going to bed, obviously, with one of them whom he liked. How their youthfulness was used to give him strength and virility is, unfortunately, not known to us and remains a medieval secret. There was no turn and, in fact, no rule in this polygamous *harem* and the king's sweet will was the final word. His queens and concubines, therefore, vied with each other to win his heart with various strategems which they could afford to muster in that age. But it was ultimately his choice. Some youthful slave-girl was always in attendance, when the king was in the *harem*, to look after his personal service, as was Anarkali.

Be that as it may, it must be remembered that Akbar never excessively indulged in wine or women and his activities in the *harem* were restrained and disciplined. His son Jehangir (1569-1627) was more sensuous and his over-indulgence in these two engagements nearly cost him his health and curtailed the span of his life.

It must be noted that the private life of the Mughal emperor was, in fact, so intermixed with his state functions that it is not possible to draw a line between the two. His state was his property which he could manage as he liked, subject of course to certain checks and balances. The king was the state and his personal needs and the needs of the state were all mixed up and were looked after by the officialdom and the people, alike. The subjects were there just to serve the state which was personified in the king and he was, therefore, designated *Annadata* (giver of the daily bread). The myth that Mughal kingship was a divine institution was firmly planted by Akbar.

He was also fond of elephant and other animal fights and hunting as outdoor amusements and pastimes. It is noteworthy that he regularly attended *jharokha* and *surya-darshan; Diwan-i-'Am* and *Diwan-i-Khass;* and *Shah Burj* even when he was travelling and living in camp, and when he was sick. Observance of these customs was binding and indispensable. His mother, sisters and women relations lived in the *harem* and one of his duties was also to take care of them.

Jehangir, his son and successor, also regularly performed *jharokha-darshan,* and other institutions of the state. He attended business in the *Diwan-i-'Am, Diwan-i-Khass* and *Shah Burj.* He spent time also in watching elephant-fights. He had instituted the Chain of Justice (*Zanjir-i-'Adl*) to impart justice to all and sundry. This was his own innovation and he spent considerable time also to the administration of justice to his people. His evenings were, however, spent in drinking sessions after which, obviously late in night, he retired to sleep. It must be noted that, though he travelled a lot and mostly lived in camp, this routine was scrupulously followed and these customs were unavoidably observed even when he was indisposed. The English ambassador, Sir Thomas Roe, who lived with him in camp for about three years, therefore, noted that his life was as regular as a clock that struck at set hours. These were the basic functions of the Mughal king which none could afford to miss.

Jehangir spent no time in meditation like his father or in prayer like his son. Instead he devoted himself to the art of painting in which he was greatly interested. Mughal painting reached its zenith under his patronage and this is his singular contribution to the arts and culture of this country.

Shah Jehan used to get up at 4 o'clock in the morning. He performed ablution at the *Abshar-i-Taufiq* (marble water-basin with fountain used for ablution) and, around day-break, said his morning prayers. Then he went to the *jharokha* which was situated in the *harem* quarters, facing east, and showed himself to the people. He followed morning prayer and *jharokha-darshan* regularly even when he was travelling in camp. After a brief sojourn in the *harem* and looking into its matters, he went to the *Diwan-i-'Am* (Hall of Public Audience) at about 10 o'clock and conducted the usual state business. After the customary inspection of the imperial horses and elephants at 11 o'clock, he went to the *Diwan-i-Khass* and conducted important work of the state, of a confidential nature with the help of his secretaries and high officers. He remained there till noon-time, when he rose for lunch. It was spread as described above in the *harem*. While Akbar dined alone, or sometimes with his most trusted friends, Jehangir and Shah Jehan dined with ladies. It was also time to inquire about the well-being of the inmates of the *harem*. After lunch, he retired to his special sleeping room, also situated in the *harem* complex, for siesta which was a regular feature of his lifestyle. At about 2 o'clock, he came out from this room, performed ablution and said his prayer. Thereafter, he went to the *Shah Burj* where he conducted extremely confidential matters of the state and gave orders. He attended the *Diwan-i-'Am* again at 4 o'clock and remained there till sunset. Thenc he went to offer his evening prayer, after which he retired to his special private chamber in the *harem* for relaxation and entertainment. As his son Aurangzeb has recorded, sweet-tongued historians, eloquent story-tellers, sweet-voiced musicians and travellers were present there. The ladies were allowed to sit there behind the *purdah* (curtain). These people entertained the king in their own way. This went on as long as he pleased. Then the assembly was dismissed and he retired to his private chamber with his ladies in attendance.

The routine was standardised and typed so thoroughly that his descendants almost followed it religiously. There was a change only when either such a devout man as Aurangzeb who completely abstained from drinking or excessive sex and devoted more time to prayers and religious activities was on the scene, or when such a debauchee as Jahandar Shah or Muhammad Shah *Rangila* was the king when most of the time was consumed in drinking; sex; music and dance; petty lowly pastimes; and filthy vices, and the grace and decency, though not the glow, glint, glitz, gloss and glamour, of the Great Mughals were thrown to the wind.

Remarkable is the fact that every activity of the Mughal King (including his *harem* and government) was recorded in black-and-white under a precise system. It began with Akbar who appointed 14 experienced and expert *Waqi'a-Nawis* (event-writers), two of whom worked daily in the rotation of 1-2, 2-3, 3-4, 4-5 and so on, so that the turn of each one came after a fortnight. Some other suitable *munshis* (clerks) were appointed to work as extras or supernumeraries, called *Kotal*, in case of absence of some one from these 14 writers, so that the record was never delayed. This system of record-making continued throughout the Mughal period until Aurangzeb (1658-1707), who probably suspicious of his own doings, abolished it.

The duty of these writers was to write down (1) the orders and (2) the doings of the king and whatever the heads of the various departments reported, e.g. what the king ate and drank; when he slept and rose; the time he spent in the *harem*; the timings of his going to general and private assemblies; nature and timings of his hunting; activities of his *Din-i-Ilahi;* the books which were read out to him; his charities and presents; grants of *mansabs* (ranks); appointments and transfers; inspection of troops and other government departments; issues of orders related to the government and despatches; receipt of ambassadors and emissaries; receipt of *peshkash* (presents); receipt of reports and minutes from various departments; hearing of petitions and award of judgements; the proceedings of general assemblies, marriages, births and indoor and outdoor games etc. covering each and every aspect of his life, private and public.

The diary was corrected, periodically, by one of the King's trusted officers. It was then placed before him for his approval. The writer then made a copy of each report, signed it and handed it over to those who required it as a voucher, when it was also signed by the *Parwanchi* (chief of the writers' department), the *Mir-'Arz* (superintendent of petitions) and by the officer who placed it before the king. This official report was then called *Yad-Dasht* (Memorandum).

The procedure of making the Imperial record did not end there. There were several copyists (*Naqal-Nawis*). They received *Yad-Dasht* and kept it with themselves and made its summary. They signed this summary and returned it, keeping the original *Yad-Dasht* with them. The summary was signed and sealed by *Waqi'a-Nawis* (event-writer), *Risala-dar* (security officer), *Mir-'Arz* (superintendent of petition) and *Darogha* (superintendent of the department) after which it was called *Ta'liqa*.

The object of this precise record making, as the contemporary historian has enumerated, was that every duty was properly performed; that there was no undue increase or decrease in any department; that dishonest officials were exposed and removed and the honest and the trustworthy were rewarded and upgraded; and that the efficient servants could work without fear, while the negligent and forgetful were checked, warned and deterred. This system helped to run the *harem* and the government in proper order and discipline and it also left a glorious record of the exalted regime for the posterity. This never happened in India, or in any other country before, and it was the Mughals' unique contribution to human progress and civilisation.

The Mughal *harem* was, in fact, a thoroughly organised institution where the inmates lived comfortably and decently. It was gorgeously furnished with carpets, curtains and furniture of sandal and ebony, and was adequately lighted. Its kitchen was efficiently maintained and served both vegetarian and non-vegetarian dishes, round the clock. Besides relishing sumptuous dishes, the Mughals were also fond of wine, opium and, above all *pan* (betel-leaf). They used perfumes on their person and incenses in the interiors. The ladies lived a regal life with taste and refinement, and with unbounded luxury. They wore the finest costumes and the costliest jewellery, and *Shah-Tus* shawls, gold brocades and pearl-strings were commonly used in the Mughal *harem*. There was ample provision for amusements and pastimes. Though the ladies lived within the four walls of the palace, under inviolable *purdah* (seclusion), gardens and tanks with canals, waterfalls and fountains were provided therein which ensured refreshing open spaces. The Mughal *harem* was, as a matter of course, situated on a river-bank (e.g. at Agra, Lahore and Delhi) or by the side of a natural lake (e.g. at Ajmer and Bari) which enabled the ladies to enjoy cool breezes, pleasant vistas and beautiful landscapes. There was no drudgery and they lived happily.

But they did not have 'family life' in the right sense of the term, and they were just part of the vast establishment of a polygamous husband. Besides the legally married wives, there were numerous concubines and slave-girls, young and beautiful, who were all attached to his bed. He alone presided over the *harem* like the proverbial 'golden cock among his gilded hens'. He enjoyed a woman exclusively, but he denied that exclusivity to her, and a woman, being a woman, could not bear it. But that was a different age, when women were sold in open market and were treated more as a commodity than human beings. Our civilisation which is living and dynamic has greatly evolved through the ages.

DETAIL OF COLOUR PLATES

Jehangir, Nur Jehan and Shah Jehan in the Harem at Mandu (1617). 18th century copy of an early 17th century original Mughal Painting

Lady offering cup of wine to Jehangir in the Harem. (early 17th century Mughal Painting)

A woman being led to Muhammad Shah 'Rangila' in the Harem. (early 18th century Mughal Painting)

A Nobleman with his Ladies in the Harem. (mid-18th century Mughal Painting)

Ladies relaxing in a Palace-Garden with music and drink. (Mughal painting, early 18th century)

Interior of a Mughal Palace. (early 18th century)

Mughal King Farrukh-Siyar (1713-19) sitting on the river-side terrace of a palace, listening to music. (early 18th century)

A Mughal Prince watching a dance performance at night. (c. 1700 A.D.)

INDEX

Abdullah Khan Mughul, 28
Abraham, 66, 69
Abshar-i-Taufiq, 210
Abu'l Fazl (Sheikh), 11, 19, 42, 44, 53, 55, 72-75, 77, 78
Abu'l Wasi, 28
Achin, 110, 122
Adam, 71
Afghanistan, 21, 61
Africa, 68
Agra, 23, 26, 37, 47, 48, 56, 57, 97, 103, 104, 177, 189, 214
Agra Fort, 12, 14, 16, 18, 19, 46, 103, 104, 158
Ahmad b. Hanbal, 69
Ahmadi, 116
Ahmedabad, 23, 103, 189
'Ain-i-Akbari, 11
Ajmer, 23, 56, 79, 80, 103, 104
Akbar (Jalalu'd-Din Muhammad), 11, 19, 23, 25-28, 33, 35,36,40-44, 47, 50, 53, 54, 71-80, 84, 98, 103, 105, 106, 108, 109, 112, 113, 119, 122, 125, 126, 130, 132, 144, 155, 160, 163-166, 168, 177, 189, 190, 192, 193, 195, 198, 207-209, 211, 212
Akbarabadi-Mahal Begum, 36
Akbari-Mahal, 16
Akbar-Namah, 72
Allahabad, 50
'Ali Quli Beg Istalju (Sher Afkun), 33, 34
Ali Rai, 30
Ali Sher Beg, 71
Allopanisad, 76
Amarkot, 79

Ambar (Khwajah), 53
Amer (Ambar, modern Jaipur), 28, 29, 41, 46
Amir Khusrau, 62, 169
Anarkali, 35, 36, 209
Arabia, 70
Arjumand Banu Begum (Mumtaz Mahal), 36
Arthashastra, 144
Asad Beg, 122-124
Asaf Khan, 58
Asia, 21, 68
Askari, 25
Asmat Begum, 51, 112
Astar-Ghach, 118
Astarabad, 71
Assyria, 64
Atagah Khan, 54
Aurangabadi-Mahal, 38
Aurangzeb, 11, 22, 38, 78-80, 104, 121, 133, 160, 193, 211, 212
Ayisha Sultan Begum Miranshahi, 25
Aziz Koka, Mirza, 25

Baba-i-Kabuli, 71, 117
Babur, 25, 26, 53, 71, 75, 91, 115, 118, 119, 132, 169, 207
Babur-Namah, 71
Badaoni, 43, 46, 73, 75-77
Badi-uz-Zaman, Mirza, 71
Bahraich, 83
Bahrayan, 111
Balkh, 71
Bargah, 185
Bari, 214
Barnabas, 67

Basrah, 111
Bega (Haji) Begum, 25, 72
Bengal, 54, 55
Bengali-Mahal, 46
Bhagwandas of Amer, Raja, 29, 42, 44
Bhakkar, 54
Bharmal Kachhwaha of Amer, Raja, 28, 41, 42, 44
Bhira (Punjab), 115
Bibi Mubarika, see Mubarika Bibi
Bible, 66
Bihar, 126
Bijapur, 122
(The) *Book of Genesis*, 66, 76
British East India Co, 41
Bukhara, 98
Burhanpur, 37

Catholic Dictionary of Theology, 67
Chaldea, 64
Chaman, 98
Chambal, 121
Chanakya, 144
Chandal-Mandal, 160
Chaupar, 165
Chenab, 103
Chess, see *Shatranj*
China, 61, 110, 123
Christ (Isa), 66, 71, 77
Chubin Raoti, 185
Cyprus, 110

Daniyal, 73

Dara, 79, 80
Daulatabadi-Mahal, 38
Daulat-Shad, Bibi, 28
Deccan, 121
Delhi, 23, 62, 214
Dhanasari, 110
Dildar Begum, 25
Dil-i-Aram, 38
Dilras Banu, 38
Din-i-Ilahi, 76, 80, 212
Diwan-i-'Am, 210, 211
Diwan-i-Khass, 208, 210, 211
Do-Ashiyana-Manzil, 185
Dohad, 79, 80

Egypt, 61, 64, 68
Ethiopia, 68
Europe, 68, 192

Fancy Bazar (*Mina-Bazar*), 156-158
Farrash-Khanah, 180
Fatehpuri Begum, 36
Fatehpur Sikri, 12, 46, 73, 76, 79, 103, 157, 165, 177, 189
Firuz Khan, Khwajasara, 57, 58, 60

Gadai, 116
Ganga, 103
Ghiyath Beg, Mirza, 33, 36
Ghiyath-i-Naqshband, 190
Goshkan, 177
Greece, 61
Gujarat, 110

Gulbadan, 25, 71
Gulal-bar, 185
Gul-Barg Barlas, 25
Gulnar Aghacha, 25
Gulrukh Begchik Begum, 25
Gunwar Bibi, 25
Gwalior, 56, 83

Hamida Banu Begam, 25, 72
Hanzalah, 71
Har Rai of Jaisalmer (Rawal), 42
Hardwar, 103
Hawkins, see William Hawkins
Herodotus, 61
Hilal, Khwajah, 56
Hilalabad, 56
Hindal, Mirza, 25, 72
Hindustan, 55, 91, 126, 191
Hira Bai (Zainabadi-Mahal), 38
Hisar Firoza, 83
Hud, 71
Hul-Hul Aniga, 117, 118
Humayun, 25, 26, 53, 71-73, 119, 132, 193, 207
Husain Chak of Kashmir, 30
Husain Mirza, Sultan, 71

'Ibadat-Khanah, 76, 77
Ibrahim 'Adil Shah, II, 122
Ibrahim Lodi, 91
Idris, 71
India, 53, 61, 68, 70, 80, 111, 160, 169, 177, 207
Iran, 124, 177

Islam Shah, 54
I'tibar Khan (Khwajasara), 27, 56, 57, 59
I'tibar Khan Nazir, 53
I'timad Khan, 54, 59
I'timadpur, 55
'Itri-i-Jahangiri, 112

Jagat Singh, 30
Jahandar, 30
Jahandar Shah, 212
Jaisalmer, 30, 44
James Tod, Col., 41
Jamuna, see Yamuna
Java, 110
Jawahar-Khanah, 203, 205
Jehangir, 11, 23, 28-30, 34, 43, 46, 47, 49, 50, 53, 55-58, 75, 79, 80, 103, 104, 112, 119, 124, 132, 156, 158, 165, 205, 206, 209-211
Jehangiri-Mahal, 16,
Jehangir-Jas-Chandrika, 57
Jerusalem, 70
Jharokha, 210, 211
Jodhbai (*Jagat-Gosain*), 29, 42, 47, 48, 50

Ka'aba, 78
Kabul, 23, 53, 71-73, 79, 98, 103, 117, 177
Kalyan Mal of Bikaner, Raja, 42, 44
Kalyan Mal of Jaisalmer, Raja, 30
Kama-Sastras, 130
Kamran, 25, 73
Karamsi, 30
Karttikeya, 46
Kasganj (Etah), 103

Kashmir, 23, 30, 83, 98, 103, 180, 194, 198
Keshavdas, 57
Kesu Das Rathor, Raja, 30
Khandesh, 28, 30
Khan-i-'Alam, 124
Khan-i-'Azam, Nawab, 122, 123
Khanwa, 119
Khurram (Shah Jehan), 29, 47, 57, 75, 79
Khusrau (son of Jehangir), 29, 49, 56, 57, 75, 79
Khusrau, 116
Khuzistan, 177
Khwaja Dost-Khawand, 116
Khwajah Hasan, 29, 30
Khwajah Jahan-i-Kabul, 30
Kirman, 177
Kuan Kamal Khan, 104
Kurkyaraq (*Karkaraq Khanah*), 189

Lahore, 23, 35, 58, 75, 79, 103, 177, 189, 198, 214
Lahauri, 18
Langar Khan, 116
Lut, 71

Madar Gate (Agra), 56
Madina, 61, 122
Mahal-i-Ilahi (Birbal's Palace), 157
Maham Begum, 25
Mah-Chuchak Begum, 25
Malika-i-Jehan, 30, 36
Mandu, 23, 103
Man Bai (Shah Begum), 29, 42, 49, 50
Man Singh, 57

Mqsud 'Ali, 54, 55
Maryam-uz-Zamani, 47, 51
Ma'suma Sultan Begum, 25
Mathnawi Shahr-Ashub, 62
Maywa-Jan, 25
Mecca, 61, 70, 122
Meer Ali, Mrs, 92
Mihr-un-Nisa (Nur Jehan), 33, 34, 36
Mina-Bazar, see Fancy Bazar
Miran Mubarak Shah, 28, 54
Mirim, 116
Mirza Quli, 116
Moses (Musa), 65, 71
Mubarak Chak of Kashmir, 30
Mubarika, Bibi, 25
Muhammad (Prophet), 71, 76
Muhammad Akbar, 38
Muhammad 'Azam, 38
Muhammadi, 116
Muhammad-i-Qasim Barlas, 117
Muhammad Kambakhsh, 38
Muhammad Khan, 54
Muhammad Mua'zzam, 38
Muhammad Mumin Mirza, 71
Muhammad Shah Rangila, 212
Muhammad Sultan, 38
Mulla Asad (Mahfuz Khan), 158
Mumtaz Khan, see I'tibar Khan Khwajasara
Mumtaz Mahal, 37, 51, 129
Muntakhabu't-Tawarikh, 77
Murad, 73
Muzaffar Husain, 30

Nadira Begum (Sharf-un-Nisa Begum, Anarkali), 35
Na'man, 116
Nar-Gul, 25
New Guinea, 68
Nimlah, 83
Nizamuddin Ahmad (Khwajah), 44, 72, 73, 75
Nuh, 71
Nur Jehan Begum, 30, 33, 34, 36, 58, 112, 168, 194
Nur-un-Nisa, 30

Observations on the Musalmans of India, 92
Orissa, 126

Panchisi, 165
Palestine, 62
Panhan, 105
Panipat, 91
Paul, 67
Pelsaert (Francois), 27, 30
Persia, 61, 124, 177
Phul Malik, 54
Punjab, 54, 105

Qandahar, 53, 72, 98
Qandahari Begum, 36
Qasim-i-Ali, 116
Qasim Khan Namakin, 56
Quran, 10, 62, 69
Qush-Nadur, 117

Rahmat-un-Nisa (*Nawab Bai*), 38
Rai Singh of Bikaner, Rai, 29, 42

Rajasthan, 41
Rajauri, 83
Rajputana, 41
Raju of Rajauri, Raja, 38
Ramchandra Bundela, 30
Raniwas (Jodhbai's Palace), 157
Rauh Dam, 116
Ravi, 103
Red Fort (Delhi), 103
Rubaiyat-Peshawaran, 62
Runkuta, 56
Ruqayyah Begam, Sultan, 28

Sabzwar, 177
Sahib-i-Jamal, 29
Sa'id Khan Chaghtai, 55
Sa'id Khan Ghakkar, 29
Salih, 71
Saliha Banu Begum, 30
Salim (Jehangir), 33-36, 42, 73-75, 78, 79
Salima Begum, Sultan, 28
Sam, 71
Samarqand, 71, 98
Sanga, Rana, 119
Sarjar, Mirza, 30
Shah Bibi, 25
Shah Abbas, 124
Sher Afkun, see 'Ali Quli Beg Istalju
Shaham Agha, 25
Shah Begum, see Man Bai
Shah-Burj, 208, 210
Shahi Kutub-Khanah (The Imperial Library), 166

Shah Jehan, 11, 18, 19, 36, 47, 57, 58, 103, 104, 121, 132, 158, 165, 210, 211
Shah Mansur, 109
Shah Nawaz Khan, 36
Shah Nawaz Khan Safawi, 38
Shahriyar, 30, 58
Shah-Zada, 117, 118
Shatranj (Chess), 163
Shis, 71
Shu'aib, 71
Sikandara (Agra), 47, 57
Sirhindi Begum, 36
Sohagpura, 26
Soron, 103
South India, 110
Sulaiman, 71
Sultan-un-Nisa Begum, 29
Sylhet, 55
Syria, 61

Taj Mahal, 37
Tamarik (Valley), 71
Tardi Beg, 117, 118
Tardi Muhammad Qibchaq, 116, 117
Tarikh-i-Ilahi, 76
Tavernier (J.B.), 18
Thomas Roe, Sir, 210
Tibet, 30
Timothy, 67
Tingri-Quli, 116
Turan, 177
Turkey, 61, 110

Udaipuri Bai (Mahal), 38
Udai Singh (Mota Raja of Jodhpur), 29, 42
Ujjain, 23
Umar Sheikh, Mirza, 71
Urta-Bagh, 72

Waqi'a-Nawis, 212
Wazir Khan, 27
William Hawkins, 205, 206

Yadgar Nasir, Mirza, 72
Yahya, 71
Yaman, 122
Yamuna (River), 26, 103, 104
Yusuf, 71
Yusuf-i-'Ali, 116

Zainab, 25
Zainabadi-Mahal, see Hira Bai
Zakariya, 71
Zanjir-i-'Adl (The Chain of Justice), 210
Zeb-un-Nissa, 160
Zirbad, 110

The Sufi Shrine of Ajmer

Laxmi Dhaul

Hazrat Khwaja Moinuddin Chisti's tomb lies in Ajmer in Rajasthan. He was one of the greatest Sufi saints and his Dargah is a centre of pilgrimage for thousands of people of all faiths. The Dargah complex is a conglomeration of various buildings, places of worship and tombs of various people built over the last 750 years. Various Sufi rituals, the annual Urs and daily ceremonies held at the Dargah are a fascinating mix of different customs. Miracles and prayers answered are a feature of the Ajmer Dargah and this alone attracts thousands of devotees daily. The patronage of the Mughal, Rajput and Maratha emperors and kings have added tremendous variety and colour to the shrine as it is today.

This book though based on the life of a Saint of the thirteenth century is extremely relevant even today for it deals with mysticism, love, unity, sacrifice, spirituality and secularism. The Saint's preachings are vibrant, even today, as they strengthen the fabric of love and unity amongst diverse faiths.

Laxmi Dhaul is a sceince graduate from St Xavier's College. Mumbai and an M.Sc in Biochemistry from Mumbai University. She lives in Mumbai and is currently writing a book on Shri Eklingji, the Shiva shrine near Udaipur.

Jaipur 10 Easy Walks

Dharmendar Kanwar

The first book of its kind, it gives the tourist a chance to explore the famed lanes of Jaipur. See the well planned streets from close quarters and discover the city's architectural beauty in its monuments — havelies, temples and other traditional buildings, its carefully preserved heritage, its culture and craft skills. The streets are crowded and lively and there is much to see and enjoy — the marble statue maker, the dyer and printer, the bangle seller, the *mithaiwala,* the artist and the jeweller... This book gives the reader a chance to explore a totally different aspect of Jaipur and shows that there is more to this 276 – year – old city than the famous Amber Fort and Hawa Mahal.

Dharmendar Kanwar studied at Maharani Gayatri Devi Girls Public School and went to University in Jaipur. She started her writing career immediately after finishing school. In the late Eighties, she took to travel writing and was resident editor of *Rajasthan Atithi* for a year. She authored *Rajasthan,* a coffee table book besides writing several brochures on Rajasthan that won national awards. She was awarded the Best Travel Writer (English) for 1993-94 by the Government of Rajasthan. She has edited, designed and published *Gourmet's Gateway* by Rajmata Gayatri Devi, co – authored *Delhi Agra Jaipur,* written *Fifty Years of Rajasthan Police* and *Enduring Grace,* a biography of Rajmata Gayatri Devi.

Temples & Erotic Art of Khajuraho

R. Nath

For centuries, the erotic sculptures of the temples of Khajuraho have thrilled human imagination. Do these sculptures merely ornament them, or can their presence be attributed to some other reason? All these questions related to the architecture of these temples have been answered in an extremely simple and lucid style. Supported by black and white and colour plates and drawings, this study of the art and architecture of Khajuraho will be appreciated by both the layman and the serious scholar.

Professor R. Nath has worked at more than 50 ancient and medieval sites of India and with his extensive knowledge of Sanskrit and Persian, has authored several books, monographs, research papers and articles. Currently he lives and works from Agra.